The Disappearance of Melanie Hall

Pete Dove

Published by Trellis Publishing, 2021.

THE DISAPPEARANCE OF MELANIE HALL

First edition. July 11, 2021.

ISBN: 979-8224372362

Written by Pete Dove.

THE DISAPPEARANCE OF MELANIE HALL

PETE DOVE

A Motorway for a Grave

Despite the fumes from lorries and the whine of speeding cars, much of the M5 is a pleasant enough road to drive. Once the heavy traffic of Birmingham is left behind, the road cuts through the gentle hills of the Malverns and central Gloucestershire. Two splendid bridges are soon spied crossing a major river and taking traffic into the Principality of Wales, thus saving drivers a long detour to the north.

This major motorway runs from England's second city, Birmingham, in the Midlands, the central industrial heartland of the country, down to the holiday destinations of the South West, including Somerset and the chocolate box villages of Devon. The M5, six lanes of speeding traffic, passes through just one other major city on its route – Bristol, which sits high up on the Severn Estuary, the wide river mouth which separates England from south Wales.

Clifton, Bristol's most exclusive suburb, is cut into the hills and another long bridge soars over the tidal estuary below. Then the hills become bigger, and holiday resorts begin to be highlighted on brown motorway signage. To the west sit the highlands of Exmoor, home of the mythical beast and real cream teas, and, later, the even more dramatic Dartmoor, whose barren moors are glorified in the works of writers such as Daphne Du Maurier and Sir Arthur Conan Doyle.

But the road is not all beauty. Its Thornberry section is one such less than attractive place. Close to Gordano, the unlovely services recently renamed Michaelwood, here the views tell of the working life of the Severn and its confluence with Avonmouth. Docks and heavy industry sit on the muddy banks, and the temptation is to push the accelerator down a little further, and pick up extra speed to leave the litter strewn verges behind.

On October 5th, 2009 workmen were carrying out maintenance here along the northwards side of the M5, clearing the undergrowth, when they came across some thin, cheap black plastic bin bags, tied across the top with building twine. Inside were bones and a skull. After thirteen years of fear over what had happened to Melanie Hall, the worst news was confirmed. These were the remains of her body. Although she had officially been declared dead, five years earlier in 2004, hope remained in her family that, by some miraculous chance, their daughter might turn up alive one day. That painful desire was wiped out by the discovery of those carelessly discarded bin bags.

'We had a young, vibrant daughter,' said her father, Steve, in a news conference soon after the gruesome discovery. 'Happy, with a future in front of her. Today we have a bag of bones, discarded by the side of the motorway,' the bitterness, the fury in his voice was impossible to ignore.

'It's taken thirteen years for us to actually find her, and now we're relying very much on everybody to come up with some information to answer the questions, who, and why?' added Patricia

Despite the deeply advanced state of decay of Melanie's body, it was still possible to identify a cause of death from the remains. Severe head injuries. A ring was discovered with her, and nearby in the undergrowth a set of rusting keys to a Ford motor vehicle.

But nothing more.

Melanie had spent the evening enjoying herself at a night club in Bath, in the South West of England. Cadillacs was a popular spot with twenty somethings back in the dying years of the old millennium. A little more upmarket, a little more sophisticated than the typical attraction of its kind, it drew a slightly older clientele than many such establishments. It was a June evening, early summer when the days are long, and warm. Inside, barely lit plush pink walls were offset by retro style metallic tables and round backed high bar stools, like a gaudy US diner, spotlights glaring into the eyes of dancing merry makers and the music pumped.

At around 1.10 am Melanie was sitting on one such stool on the edge of the dancefloor in the dimly lit cavern. That was most probably the last time that, other than her killer, anybody saw her alive. Although, later, unconfirmed reports that she lingered outside in the morning's early hours arose. The night had not turned out as planned for the vibrant blond. She had intended to stay the night with her boyfriend, Philip Karlbaum on 8th June, and her mother had dropped her off at his home the night before. Karlbaum was a doctor at the same hospital in which Melanie worked, and they had met on the orthopedic ward. At the time of her disappearance, the couple had been dating for just three weeks.

They were certainly living life to the full in those early summer months. On June 7th, 1996, which was a Friday, they had travelled together to a party held by a colleague, and then slept in late the following morning. Next, they headed into Bristol where, it seems, Melanie purchased the blue dress she was wearing at the nightclub from where she disappeared. They had gone to a busy barbeque before leaving with another couple to go to the nightclub. It was there that matters began to get messy.

It seems as though Philip took Umbridge at his girlfriend dancing with another man in the busy nightclub. In fact, according to witnesses, he departed in a 'jealous rage.' It was unclear initially whether or not she had actually been dancing with another man, and who that man might have been. Nevertheless, an argument ensued, and Philip left, upset. Melanie remained behind with the friends, who were unaware of the disagreement. It was they who, at 1.10 in the morning, found her sitting on a stool. They told her that they were leaving, and wished her goodnight, believing that Philip was still in the nightclub, just elsewhere at that time. Later, the man with whom she had been dancing was identified, but he was never a suspect in the police's enquiries

It was three days on that her increasingly worried mother reported her as missing, after she failed to turn up for work.

Melanie was just twenty-five years old at the time of her disappearance, and police immediately suspected the worst. There seemed to be no reason for her to willingly take herself off.

'She had everything to look forward to, she was young, attractive, had so much to look forward to in her life and I'm sure she wouldn't have done this of her own free will,' said her devastated mother, Patricia, at the time of her disappearance. 'If she is still alive, I would just like to know where she is, and we could just put our minds at rest.'

'She had so many things to do in life, and she was denied them,' added her still clearly devastated father some time later, following years of determined, but halting, police enquiries.

For example, three years prior to the discovery of her bones, police had launched a campaign to find a particular white Volkswagen Golf, the sort of sporty hatchback very popular on British roads, especially with younger – often male - drivers in the 1980s and 90s. As with so many other leads upon which the family, and investigators, have pinned their hopes over the years, whichever road they hoped the Golf would lead them down, it came to an abrupt halt, another dead end.

'People out there know what happened and have not come forward. We would just ask that they find the moral fiber within them to come forward, we need help,' said her father in 2016, appearing on the BBC TV true crime program, Crimewatch.

Melanie was a bright girl, successful at school but a home girl, who stayed in her birth city of Bath to attend University at its well-regarded institution. After four years of study she graduated with a Psychology degree of which she was extremely proud. She had spent a year following that graduation in 1995 sorting out in her mind what she wished to do with her life. She was working as a clerical officer at the Royal United Hospital in the city when she went missing.

She got on well with her older sister, Dominique, as well as with her parents. She also loved her hometown city. The entire family did, father Steve even serving for a time as Chairman of the City's non-league soccer team.

Whilst not perhaps London, or Edinburgh, Bath is one of the more expensive cities in Britain, nevertheless, and difficult for a young person to gain a foothold in the housing market. Melanie was still living at home with her parents when she disappeared.

It is a city of stunning, curved, Georgian terraces, where houses can cost millions of pounds. It is also of historical significance, and its Roman remains attract millions of tourists per year. In fact, Melanie, Steve and Patricia lived just a few miles outside of the city itself, in Bradford upon Avon, a small town lying on the beautiful banks of the river seven miles to the south of Bath. This town too enjoys stunning architecture, but without the bustle and hustle of its larger neighbor, which can detract from its own attractions for people who live there.

At the time of her disappearance the attractive, bobbed-blond young woman was wearing a light blue silk summer dress with a pale cream jacket. She carried a black shoulder length bag, and wore black slip on mule shoes, with firm, blocked heels. In the bag were her check book and bank cards. Neither her clothing, nor the contents of her handbag, have ever been found.

'An incident like this is life changing, and you're never the same afterwards. You're a different person,' said Steve, for whom there are constant reminders that he will never see his daughter again. 'She's left a very big gap really, for us both.'

Over the almost a quarter of a century – as long as she lived before her disappearance – since Melanie went missing, police had picked up a number of leads. Enough for them to arrest no less than eleven suspects. However, none of these arrests has led to a charge. Those arrests are a second aspect to the case which must not be forgotten. The trauma Melanie faced, and that her family and friends will still endure until a culprit can be found and some kind of closure achieved, are tragic. Not equally, but nonetheless very significantly, the lives of those eleven men arrested, accused of outrageous acts of violence, subject to fear and threat, have also been damaged. Some more so than others, but all to an extent that will remain with them, and their families, forever.

Maybe a more sympathetic body than the British police, the Avon and Somerset branch in this case, could have dealt with their enquiries more effectively, and in a way that left less collateral damage. But no doubt their work is hard, hard enough to make them forget that other people's lives can also be ruined by careless, or over ambitious, searches for a conclusion. Everybody wants justice, but maybe not at any cost.

Detective Superintendent Andy Bevan was leading the case in 2016. The senior detective took his moment on television back then to reveal another possible lead in the search for Melanie's killer.

'We have DNA evidence on an item that was found at the scene where Melanie's remains were found back in 2009,' he announced on national TV, speaking in that curious mix of awkward precision so favored by police officers, and especially those from Britain. Never use one word when six will suffice seems to be the underlying purpose here. Although, the slight West Country tang in his accent softened the coldness of the words. 'We're working closely with forensic scientists to establish a DNA profile,' he continued for any members of the audience whose interest had not been lost through his pedantic delivery, 'and I believe that will bring us a step closer to finding who is responsible for Melanie's murder which of course is what we all want for Melanie's family who have had to endure twenty years of pain.'

DS Bevan attempted to bring people's minds back to the time in question by showing footage of the bordello like interior of the now defunct Cadillacs, and reminding viewers that the night of Melanie's disappearance coincided with England's disappointing 1-1 draw with not very mighty Switzerland in the Euro 96 soccer championships, which the country was hosting.

At the time of writing, Detective Chief Inspector James Riccio has taken over leadership of the investigation, within his role in the force's Major Crime Investigation Team. 'As part of a nationwide appeal issued on the 20th Anniversary of her disappearance we confirmed we'd recovered DNA on an item found at the site where Melanie's body was found' he said, implying that this find, first reported on the Crimewatch Roadshow television program more than three years previously, had yet to yield any useful results. However, he had further news.

'Today,' he said, 'we're confirming the DNA traces were found on a length of blue polypropylene rope which was wrapped around thin black bin liners which had contained her body.'

'We recovered a 13-meter length of 4mm rope from the scene, made up from four separate lengths knotted together,' he went on with pedantic precision. 'In addition to the three knots joining the ropes there were four other knots on the rope. A total of seven knots.'

The product itself was of the tightly wound kind often used on building sites, and also for drawing electrical cable through trunking. It is the sort of cheap rope used which cuts at your fingers when trying to undo knots, sharp and feeling like harsh nylon.

But even with Detective Superintendent Bevan's timely reminder that Melanie had disappeared during the 1996 European soccer championships, the posers then set by the police for the public are intensely tough, and very much not the sort of detail likely to stick in a mind.

Did people know of someone who had some of that kind of rope? The answer to that is probably yes, since it is the sort of omnipresent handyman's resource found in many domestic garages, tying together random lengths of timber. However, recalling somebody whose unremarkable piece of blue rope went missing inexplicably a quarter of a century back is somewhat more of a challenge. As is, to be honest, remembering a person whose behavior changed twenty-five years ago, and has not been the same since.

However, DCI Riccio's other observations have more pertinence. 'We believe it is highly likely the person who left Melanie's body at this location (beside the motorway) was familiar with this area,' he said. 'It's likely this person would have then driven onto the northbound

M5 and either onto the next junction, or they maybe turned off at the Michaelwood Services, where they could have used the local road network, including a slip road behind the services, to head back in a southerly direction.'

However, the detective is not convinced that the person who threw out the bin bags is necessarily the same individual who killed Melanie. 'The person who deposited the body may not be the person who killed Melanie,' he said, before adding that if that was indeed what had happened then the person should come forward, not least to help offer some comfort to the victim's family.

'You've been living with a dark secret for years, but your guilt and fear is nothing compared to the enduring pain felt by Melanie's family. I want to be clear – our primary focus is on identifying the person or persons who killed Melanie.

'There are two things that are going to solve this case, maybe singly or maybe in combination' said Steve twenty years after he had last seen his daughter. 'One is the continuous development of forensic science, but also there are people out there who knew what happened.' Her parents still have on offer a reward of £50,000, along with the £10,00 being offered by the UK's Crimestoppers organization, for information which leads to the arrest and conviction of Melanie's killer or killers.

Yet although time passes taking the dreadful day Melanie disappeared further into the foggy distance, the moment is as fresh to Steve and Patricia as it was when they were still in the prime of their lives.

'In our family we will forever grieve for, and miss our lovely daughter,' he said. 'A young woman whose life stretched before her until that fateful night in June 1996, when that life was so cruelly snatched from her. She will never fulfil her life's ambitions, never marry, never have children and my wife and I will never have another grandchild.'

He paused, before adding, 'Her mother's lasting memory of her youngest daughter is the day she viewed a battered skull and a few broken bones in the coroner's office at Portishead.'

A framed photograph from the seventies still sits in the Hall's front room, black and white and of a very young Melanie and her older sister, Dominique, in identical, flowery dresses looking left, presumably at their mother or father as the shot is framed. It is of its day, posed to look natural yet marking a happy moment which haunts them still, a reminder of what they have lost.

During the subsequent investigations, the police certainly put considerable energy into finding Melanie's killer. They interviewed more than 2000 people in an attempt to gain a lead, as well as putting out a number of appeals on national TV. It was through this process that the eleven, mostly unfortunate, men were identified as strong suspects and arrested. They too becoming additional victims in this unpleasant matter.

Among these inadvertent quarries were a 37-year-old who actually confessed to the crime in 2009. However, after undergoing psychological assessments, prosecutors concluded that he could not have committed the offence. A year later two more men were arrested and released on bail Because the identification of these men was kept secret, and police information has throughout been sketchy, it is impossible to say whether the men's arrests were connected, although the fact that the second of these handed himself in shortly after the first was questioned suggests that they may have been. Perhaps the closest the police came to actually landing a charge was against a 44-year-old man who was arrested in Bath in November 2013. A property, presumably his home, was searched, but no further evidence came to light and the man was eventually removed as a suspect in the police department's enquiries.

Melanie's murder has often been linked to other crimes committed in the south of England. One of the most notorious of these was the killing of a young estate agent, Suzy Lamplugh, some years before. While the person suspected of having murdered her, John Cannan, was in prison at the time Melanie went missing, and was therefore ruled out of their enquiries, police believed for a while that a former cellmate, Christopher Clark, could have important information for them.

Even better known is the search for the Batman Rapist, so called because a baseball cap bearing a logo of the superhero was found at the site of one of his attacks. This man is still at large. Operation Eagle, the investigation to try to find the culprit, is the longest running serial rape investigation in Britain. The rapist attacked at least seventeen women in Bath from 1991 and he is believed to have been foiled in an attack just hours before Melanie was last seen. A woman was carjacked at knife point in the same area of the city as Cadillacs, but she fought back and despite being wounded, managed to escape.

Further, it is thought by the police that this attacker possesses the kind of personality that would react angrily to a failure of the kind described above. In 2000, police put out an appeal on the same Crimewatch series as they have used in trying to find Melanie's attacker. However, after the show had aired, two attacks were made by the man. Whilst they could have been copycat attacks, it seems unlikely, and police believe that the criminal was taunting them for their actions.

In fact, police do have a strong suspect in this case. An unnamed diplomat's son was put forward by a caller to the program, and when police followed up this lead, they discovered that the diplomat's time working abroad coincided with periods during which the rapist had been quiet. However, unsurprisingly given the secretive nature of the upper echelons of the British establishment, although the police's enquiries took them abroad to countries in which the diplomat had served, information went cold. Not denied, or disproved, note, just no longer reported.

Certainly, they are big 'ifs', but if Melanie had been the victim of a rapist known to operate in the area, and that rapist did come from a family with substantial political weight, it would not be unknown for such an occurrence to be covered up. Maybe that is the reason that Melanie's death remains unsolved, and later police actions, such as with regards to DNA on the blue rope, go cold so quickly. Such a premise is, of course, speculation.

The authorities have ruled out links to some other crimes of the time, such as those committed by convicted killer Christopher Halliwell who murdered at least two women. However, one they have not denied ties Melanie's murder to one of the most infamous killers in British history, up there with the Yorkshire Ripper and Harold Shipman in notoriety if not actual volume of murders.

Levi Bellfield is a multiple rapist and murderer who is serving whole life sentences for a number of murders committed shortly after Melanie disappeared. He is best known for abducting, raping, torturing and eventually murdering thirteen-year-old Millie Dowler, who disappeared in 2002. That crime, obscene as it was in its own right, led to two startling revelations that damaged the reputation of the British police and the print media to such an extent that the stain remains today. A stain that stretches all the way up (or down) to the highest echelons of British politics. If Bellfield was involved in Melanie's death, and again this is no more than speculation (yet speculation which, unlike other theories, has not been denied) this could be something that those in power do not want raised again, for fear of bringing the blight associated with Millie's death back to public attention.

After the teenager went missing, her family believed she was still alive. This was because messages were disappearing off her phone. As incredibly as this appears, it later turned out that a gutter press type national newspaper, The News of the World – a part of the Rupert Murdoch media empire – had employed a private detective to hack the phones of the rich and famous. Including a young girl known outside of her immediate circle only because of what had happened to her. The newspaper had actually deleted messages from her full inbox, information which the police might have used to help catch her killer, or even find Millie if she were still alive, in the hope that new messages might be sent which would form the basis for a front page story. Even worse, it later emerged that Surrey police were aware of this, were allowing it and had even discussed the case, at senior level, with the newspaper.

Subsequently, the paper was closed down, and celebrities began to discover that their phones too had been hacked. The Levison Report was launched by an apparently shocked Government, meant to investigate the propriety of press actions, but its findings were never fully published, and it was widely believed that the report, which overran by years, had been subject to political interference.

Good reason for the authorities to want to avoid confirming a link between Bellfield, Millie's killer, and Melanie.

Still, though, such theories are no more than guesswork. There are some who will believe that they are no more than extreme conspiracy theories, seeking to find artificial drama to boost a tragedy which is sufficient story in itself. Others will consider it strange that police have dismissed links to some other crimes but not others, and have never managed to discover more about Melanie's killer when her body was deposited, albeit wrapped in bin bags, by the side of one of the nation's most major arterial routes.

They will also wonder about the incredibly high number of people not just listed as suspects, but actually arrested. Then released, without charge. It is almost as though there is a wish to either draw attention to the case... or divert it away from related matters.

Yet for all of the potential for the death of Melanie Hall to be one which is linked to wider concerns, it cannot be forgotten that, most importantly, this is the killing of a young women, with a family, whose future was never permitted to develop.

'I take stock,' said Steve, encompassing what it is like to live with a family whose existence is now dominated by the death of his daughter, who have been unable to move forwards with their lives for nearly twenty five years. 'A daughter who is dead, a wife who just stares at the wall, a sister who struggles to get her day together, a one hundred year old grandmother who sits in a home with soft memories and a father who puts it all in a box and tries to shut the lid. So, we all carry on.'

CHRISTINA MARCUM

The couples who commit murder together are not so rare. Of course, there is always a leader and a follower in those instances. But what happens when the law enforcement cannot pinpoint the blame on a single person and determine which one was the killer and who was the accomplice? The case of Christina Marcum and her ex-fiance Jason Singleton is a perfect example because each of them put the blame on the other person. It is still unclear what exactly happened on that January night in 2011, but both are locked up and serving their sentences.

Early life

Christina Tompkins was born in 1983 in Georgetown, Kentucky. While her early life was fairly normal, Christina's parents got divorced soon after she was born. However, Christina did still spend a lot of time with both of her parents, and she learned how to use them in order to get what she wanted. Christina was a spoiled child and saying no to her was impossible. Her divorced parents played along, feeling guilty for the fact that they are not living as a standard family anymore. It is possible that the pleasing nature of her parents made her into a violent person she became once she grew up. Christina was used to getting away with anything, so her romantic relationships were very volatile and filled with drama.

Christina met Jason E. Singleton in 2008 and the two fell madly in love immediately. She already had a young daughter from a previous love interest. The relationship was moving forward fast and the couple moved in together pretty quickly. Christina Tomkins and Jason Singleton lived at 110 Forest Hill Drive in Richmond, Kentucky and they appeared to have a typical relationship full of love and affection. But things got sour in just a couple of months because Christina would lose her temper often. She was used to getting anything she wanted, so whenever Jason told her no, Christina would physically attack him. This toxic romance lasted for years even though the law enforcement were aware of the couple and their constant fights.

The breakup

Jason Singleton and Christina Tompkins were in a relationship for two years. They even got engaged during that time and planned to marry soon. However, in September of 2010, Christina assaulted Jason and caused him a head injury after she saw him look at another woman. Jason realized that it is time to move on and he broke up the engagement. It was obvious that Christina would continue to physically attack him whenever she got a chance and that the married life with her would be a nightmare. Jason Singleton contacted the police on the night of the assault and reported the incident.

The court granted him an emergency protective order against Christina, meaning that she couldn't come near him during the duration of her trial. Christina Tompkins was in a courtroom in October of 2010. She was charged with an assault because Christina threw a cellphone directly into Jason's head on the night when the argument happened. There was no excuse for her fits of jealousy so it comes as no surprise to find out that Christina pleaded guilty to the assault.

She was released from the custody, determined to stay away from Jason Singleton. Christina couldn't control her behavior when she was near him, so she thought that a change of scenery would do her good. She remembered her old boyfriend from high school and contacted him as soon as she was out of the jail. Nick Marcum still had feelings for Christina, so he welcomed her back into his life even though the two of them lost contact years ago.

Moving on

It didn't take Christina Tompkins long to move on completely. As a matter of fact, she married Nick Marcum only two weeks after being released from the jail. She also changed her last name to Marcum. It seems like the couple had a normal relationship, but Christina was still obsessed with her ex-fiancé. She was hurt by their unexpected breakup and the fact that Jason Singleton involved the law enforcement. Christina would start talking to Nick Marcum about Jason, and it looked like she didn't keep any secrets from her husband.

Jason Singleton didn't waste any time either. He started going out with his friends frequently, determined to leave his ex-fiancée in the past. He met Angela Frazier on December 17th, 2010 at a local strip club where she worked. She was twenty-five years old at the time, and the two of them were smitten with each other. Jason was prone to impulsive behavior so he suggested Angela that they should get married right away. Angela said yes, and they tied the knot on December 20th, 2010. The newlyweds moved into the house he used to share with Christina on Forest Hill Drive.

Christina Marcum was shocked to hear that her fiancé moved on. She expected that he would pine for her. But the thing that sent her overboard was the fact that Jason brought his bride to their old home. Christina didn't like that because she still saw that house as her own. As a matter of fact, her belongings were still inside because she didn't get a chance to get them after the unexpected breakup. She confided in her friends that she thought what Jason did was wrong and that she would get her way eventually.

The abuse

Unhappy with the recent marriage of her ex-fiancé, Christina decided to forget all about the court orders and get back into his life.

It was the end of December 2010 when she started driving up to the house in the early morning hours, parking in the driveway and honking until Jason came out to speak to her. Angela was not completely familiar with the complex relationship Jason and Christina had, but she knew that the woman in front of their home was his ex-fiancee. Angela thought that Christina was overreacting because of their marriage.

Christina's torment continued in the form of constant phone calls. She stopped with the honking but would not stay off the phone. She would call Singleton residence for at least twenty to thirty times each day, regardless of the hour. She would threaten Angela over the phone if the woman answered. Christina was going off the rails, and her friends noticed that something was very wrong. She would often bring up Angela in everyday conversations, and tell everyone that she will hurt Jason's wife.

In the end, the police were contacted at least six times over the course of a couple of weeks after Angela and Jason got married. One eyewitness saw Christina breaking the windows on the house, causing damage to the property. Christina's husband was worried about her mental state, and she confessed to him that she urinated on the front porch of her ex-fiancé's house. However, there were no arrests after each and every incident which allowed Christina to run free and continue her torture.

The first serious incident happened on January 14th, 2011 when panicked Angela Singleton contacted the police, saying that Christina Marcum is standing in front of the house, refusing to leave, and making threats. Angela also mentioned that Christina damaged her car. All of this was happening at 02:30 AM. At 08:10 AM on the same day, Jason called 911 and said that Christina got into their house and that he is trying to force her out of it. Apparently, she spent the entire night in the close vicinity of the Singleton residence, making threats, and trying to find a way to enter their home.

Two days later, on January 16th, 2011, Angela once again contacted the law enforcement, informing them that her husband Jason told her not to come back home for her own safety and that he had installed a new lock on the house in order to keep Christina out. A police patrol was dispatched to the Singleton residence because they wanted to make sure Angela got out of the house safely. Her friend came to pick her up, so the police simply left. It appeared that Angela is alright and that Jason can handle the situation on his own.

It was clear that something sinister would happen eventually, but no one could have predicted the brutality of the crime that followed. Christina was reaching her boiling point but it seemed like Jason was not doing a thing in order to calm her down.

The discovery of the car and the body

On the evening of January 17th, 2011, Angela's mother Nancy contacted the local law enforcement saying that she hadn't heard from her daughter for a couple of days. That was very unlike her, so Nancy was worried that something happened to Angela. Two hours after they got the call from Nancy Canada, Lexington Police Department was informed that a vehicle was on fire. It was on Interstate 75 in Fayette County, and the police officers drove there immediately.

The car was badly burned and it was obvious from the fire patterns around the motor that someone intentionally tried to destroy the vehicle. However, the majority was still intact, and when the police officers ran the plates through their database, they discovered that the burned car belonged to Angela Frazier. The woman was nowhere near the scene, and her whereabouts were still unknown. But the officers suspected that there was more to the story.

On January 19th, 2011, a local resident discovered trash bags on his property on Tattler Branch Road, Valley View. He was immediately suspicious and after a closer examination, the man determined that there were body parts inside. He contacted the police, and they were on the scene in a couple of minutes. The officers collected the evidence, and a medical examiner confirmed that the body parts belonged to Angela Frazier. The police did find the missing woman, but they needed to determine what really happened to her.

Officer Bubba Botkin was among the first ones who arrived at the scene of the crime. He was familiar with the missing person case and was aware that the Singletons contacted the police several times in the last couple of weeks. However, he would later say: *"I felt strongly that Jason Singleton, the victim's husband, was responsible for the murder."* After confirming through the fingerprint analysis that the dismembered body parts really did belong to Angela Frazier, the police knew that they had to find the murder scene. They immediately got a warrant to search the Singleton residence. But before they could get to 110 Forest Hill Drive, the police department received a call about an ongoing hostage situation involving Singleton.

Jason Singleton was holding four people at a gunpoint in Somerset, and the local police were negotiating with him at the time. After fifteen minutes of talk, Jason agreed to surrender. One officer who was at the scene heard Singleton murmur to himself that he wanted to be killed by the police in the standoff. But that didn't happen, and the situation was resolved without any additional victims. Once he arrived at Somerset Police Department, the detectives interview Jason right away. He was willing to talk and told the officers that he would provide them with the details as long as they promise him that they would give Christina Marcum a deal.

Another detail that was noted right away was the fact that Jason Singleton smelled strongly of smoke. Knowing that Angela's car was burned a couple of days before, they immediately connected Jason Singleton with that crime. Not to forget that his own vehicle was filled with black residue which was probably from the fire. It was evident that he was near an open flame fairly recently, and there was only one arson reported in the area at that time. But finding out where Angela was killed was a priority right now. A couple of police officers drove to the Singleton residence in order to make sure no one was there and unlock all of the doors so that the crime scene investigation unit could move around easily.

Once they parked in front, they noticed that the garage door was up and that a large kitchen knife was laying there in the middle of the space. Once they got inside, the officers were hit by a strong smell of burnt materials. The walls were black in certain areas, and it appeared that Jason or Christina tried to incinerate something inside of the house. The living room carpet had a huge hole in the middle that was clearly cut out recently. An electric saw was nearby, suggesting that was the tool that was used to remove the flooring and perhaps to dismember a body as well. The crime scene investigation unit collected numerous physical evidence, including trash bags, knives, an electric saw, pieces of carpet that contained blood evidence, as well as the drain traps. It was believed that Angela's body was cut up in the living room and that Jason or maybe Christina tried to clean up the murder scene.

The autopsy results

Christina Marcum was interviewed by the police on January 20th, 2011. She was not very forward and did not tell the detectives that Jason Singleton harmed Angela Frazier right away. But after a couple of hours, she opened up and confessed that Jason told her he strangled Angela. Detective Brian Reeder was in charge of the questioning and Christina told him the following: *"I'm not saying that I'm perfect. I'm not by no means. But I'm saying I was in the wrong place at the wrong time. Absolutely the worst place at the wrong time. And I did what I could do to stop it from happening. And there was nothing I could do."*

Christina begged the investigators not to tell Jason that she was interviewed. Christina claimed that she was scared for her own life because Jason is a big guy and could do the same to her. The strangulation part was very interesting to the investigators because they were still waiting for the medical examiner's report that would determine how Angela died. It was clear that Christina Marcum knew something about the murder.

In the meantime, Dr. Victoria Shively-Graham examined the remains found in the six trash bags. The doctor was shocked by the brutality of the crime. She wrote in the report that Angela's head showed obvious signs of injuries and that her nose was broken. She was badly beaten before her death. Additionally, her ribs were broken on both sides which could have indicated that someone was sitting on top of her. There were numerous stab wounds, as well as scratches, and bruises. However, the actual cause of death was asphyxia which meant that Angela was strangled. Her eyes were red because blood vessels popped under the pressure. Dr. Victoria Shively-Graham also added that the murderer cut Angela's tattoos off in hopes that her body would not be easily identified if discovered.

Since all of the evidence pointed to the involvement of both Christina Marcum and Jason Singleton, they both remained in the custody. But their stories were beginning to sound different, so a real challenge was ahead of the investigators. Both Marcum and Singleton had contact with the victim prior to the murder and were at the house that was also a crime scene. When he was arrested after the hostage situation, Singleton was ready to speak about the gruesome crime he committed if the police keep Christina Marcum out of the jail. So it was evident that she was involved as well. Figuring out who did what was tough but the investigators were ready to take this case to a trial.

The trial of Jason Singleton

After the arrest, both Christina Marcum and Jason Singleton were charged with the murder of Angela Frazier. Jason had an additional charge for an unlawful imprisonment that happened on the day when he was taken into custody. The couple had a set bond of $500,000 so they couldn't get out before the trial. Even though Marcum's lawyer fought to reduce the bond, the attempts were unsuccessful. Jason Singleton's trial was set for the spring of 2013. He already pleaded guilty to his previous charges and received a ten years sentence. However, the murder trial was more serious because there was a possibility of a life sentence.

As soon as Jason Singleton entered the courtroom, it was clear that he intended to tell his side of the story. Once he got to a stand, he started telling his personal statement about the events that occurred in January of 2011. He briefly mentioned Marcum's visits to the house but focused on January 16th, 2011, which is the date of the murder. Jason told the judge that he asked Angela to stay away from the house for her own safety, but that she drove back in order to get some of her belongings. Jason continued to say that Angela decided to stay for a couple of hours and she took Valium which made her sleepy. Jason was in another part of the house when he heard voices. According to him, Christina Marcum got inside, and she was arguing with Angela.

He didn't want to get involved in the fight, so Jason exited the house and lit a cigarette. He got back inside after a couple of minutes and found Angela unresponsive with Christina Marcum standing by her side. His exact words were: *"I knew Christina had expressed her desire to injure or kill Angela, and in spite of that, I still left the residence. By leaving Angela unprotected in my home, I ignored my duty to protect her and manifested an extreme indifference to the value of human life by leaving Angela Frazier Singleton defenseless with the knowledge that Christina Tompkins Marcum would likely injure or kill Angela Frazier Singleton."*

Jason continued his story by saying that he tried to revive Angela, but she was already gone. Christina then asked him to get rid of the body because she couldn't do it on her own, and that she would be caught. This would mean that Christina's little daughter would grow up without a mother. Claiming that he felt sympathetic, Jason picked up Angela's lifeless body and left it in the trunk of her own car. He then drove the vehicle to a remote location in Fayette County, planning to just leave it there. But Christina remembered that she left a boot print on Angela's body, and she feared that the detectives would connect her to the crime. So Jason got back there and took the car back to the house. It was Christina's idea to cut up the body into six pieces. Christina's plan was to leave the trash bags in random locations all over the country, but Jason didn't have time for that. Instead, he scattered the remains in Madison County.

Jason Singleton pleaded guilty to tampering with evidence by destroying, concealing and altering the body and other evidence. He was still claiming that Christina Marcum was the murderer and that he simply helped her cover up the crime. Assistant Commonwealth's Attorney Jennifer Smith did not fully believe Jason's story, but she was willing to charge him with the complicity to murder. Jason Singleton was found guilty and received a sentence of thirty years in prison.

The trial of Christina Marcum

The trial of Christina Marcum was set to begin in March 2014. She was charged with a first-degree murder, as well as with tampering with evidence and hindering prosecution. Her defense team was not willing to enter a plea deal, and they were aiming for an acquittal. A member of Christina's defense team said: *"We're not pleading guilty. She didn't do anything. You don't plead guilty when you didn't do anything."*

Ted Shouse was Christina's lead defense attorney, and he decided to present her case in a completely different light. As a matter of fact, Shouse claimed that Christina suffered from post-traumatic stress disorder which was the result of her violent relationship with Jason Singleton. The defense argued that Singleton abused Marcum during the time they were together, but somehow managed to put the whole blame on her. Assistant Commonwealth's Attorney Jennifer Smith was once again the head of the prosecution and was determined to prove that Christina Marcum was guilty without a reasonable doubt.

Smith was very familiar with the history of the relationship Marcum had with Singleton and claimed that Marcum was unpredictable, violent, and extremely jealous. Steve Romines who was one of Christina's defense lawyers added an alternative fact which was supposed to prove that Singleton was the killer. His exact quote was: *"The reason she is killed is she has ratted on the organization. The last person who told police about his crimes got cut up and put in garbage bags."* The organization he was speaking of is a ring of counterfeiters and Singleton was apparently involved with them. Angela Frasier discovered their operation and wanted to speak with the authorities. Singleton prevented that by murdering her.

The defense told the jury that Christina was not present at the house when the confrontation happened, but that she simply walked in while Jason was choking Angela. He then threatened her and forced Christina to help him dispose of the body. Christina claimed that she was truly frightened by his behavior and was terrified that she would be his next victim if she didn't comply. But Jennifer Smith was prepared for this statement as well, providing the courtroom with the evidence that the Christina and Jason communicated with each other after the murder.

As a matter of fact, Christina Marcum went to Pulaski County jail to visit Jason Singleton. She did use a fake name, but Christina also left him a little bit of money in his jail account which immediately identified her as the visitor. All of this was before his trial, so the two of them planned his defense and brainstormed different ideas. One of them included Christina seducing the lead detective in hopes that would derail his investigation. The two remained in contact at least for one year after the imprisonment, which completely debunked the defense's story of intimidation.

Jennifer Smith also mentioned the fact that Christina Marcum stalked Angela Frazier for weeks before the murder, and tortured the woman with phone calls, as well as by constantly coming over by the house. It was a good introduction to prosecution's next witness, Mariah Smith. Mariah was Christina's school friend, but the two had a falling out after the murder. Christina confided in Mariah about the murder, and when Mariah told her that she would go to the police herself, Christina stalked and threatened her. She would come to Mariah's workplace on a daily basis, screaming at the woman.

Smith closed her statement with the following words: *"Does an innocent person stalk a person for weeks? Does an innocent person lie about their involvement? Does an innocent person demand a deal before telling what they know? Does an innocent person continue to seek out the company of the very person they say choked the life out of his wife?"*

The verdict and aftermath

On March 27th, 2014, Christina Marcum was found guilty of complicity to murder, tampering with evidence and hindering prosecution. The jury deliberated for a couple of hours before reaching the verdict. She was set to spend a total of thirty years behind the bars. Steve Romines, one of Christina's defense attorneys said the following to the press after hearing the verdict: *"The evidence that points to the fact she didn't do this, they ignore. She cooperated with them on that day, and look what it got her. You ever wonder why attorneys tell people not to talk to police when they're innocent, now you know."*

Romines was resolved he would prove that Marcum is innocent and he immediately started putting together an appeal. Christina Marcum is currently serving her sentence at Kentucky Correctional Institute for Women located in Pewee Valley, Kentucky. Jason Singleton is also behind the bars in Eastern Kentucky Correctional Complex in West Liberty, Kentucky.

PSYCHO GIRL : THE TRUE STORY OF CATHERINE BIRNIE

JENA DICKENS

Catherine Margaret Harrison was born on May 23rd, 1951. Her partner, David John Birnie, was born on February 16th, 1951 and died on October 7th, 2015 by way of suicide. The duo was famously known throughout Australia as: The Killer Couple. They were from Perth, Australia and were found to have murdered four women ranging in age from 15 to 31 years old, over a span of about five weeks. Their fifth victim managed to escape through the bedroom window, while Catherine was distracted by a knock at the front door. The woman immediately ran and found help. The press referred to the heinous murders as the Moorhouse Murders. The victims were taken to Catherine and David's home located at 3 Moorhouse Street in Willagee, in Western Australia, a suburb of Perth.

Catherine was only two years old when her mother died in childbirth while giving birth to Catherine's younger brother. Her brother also died, two days later. Catherine's father, Harold, couldn't manage raising Catherine on his own at that time so she went to live with her maternal grandparents. When she was ten years old, Harold petitioned the court to receive custody of Catherine again, and he won. There always seemed to be a battle. Catherine's father didn't want her, but then wanted her, always back and forth. After Catherine was convicted of four counts of murder, it caused her father to suffer a nervous breakdown.

When Catherine was twelve years old she met a boy named David Birnie and they began dating two years later when they became teenagers. Both Catherine and David came from dysfunctional families. Their home life was chaotic and messy, literally as well as figuratively. David's mother was an alcoholic and his father was away at work the majority of the time. His father died in 1986 after battling a long illness. The house, as well as his mother, were messy and unkempt. She left her older children in charge of taking care of their younger siblings. She refused to do anything when it concerned the children and their welfare. Allegedly, David's mother would leave the refrigerator door open so that the children could eat throughout the day. David was the oldest of five children. David's school friends, as well as the local priest, deemed the family dysfunctional. The parents never prepared meals for their children, the house was always a mess, and the Priest, before marrying David's parents, said that he felt that their marriage would never lead to anything good. Little did he know how accurate his assumptions would be.

Catherine and David met through mutual friends shortly after David's family moved to the same Perth neighborhood as Catherine and her father. Catherine's father felt that David was trouble and a bad influence. Catherine had begun getting into a lot of trouble with the local police ever since the two of them met. Harold begged and pleaded with Catherine to stay away from David and stay out of trouble. Of course, this just brought the two closer. Whenever two kids are told not to do something, they go out of their way to blatantly disobey.

Even in adolescence David began exhibiting violent and perverse behavior. When David turned fifteen he dropped out of school and began working as jockey apprentice for Eric Parnham at the Ascot Race Course. While there, David would hurt the horses and also began his perverse career as an exhibitionist. David committed his first rape shortly after. By this point he had spent time in and out of jail for several charges ranging from misdemeanors to felonies. He built up a reputation around town as a sex and pornography addict.

Catherine was an accessory to a lot of crimes because of her involvement with David. They built up an extensive history of numerous charges including: breaking and entering, trespassing, unlawfully driving a motor vehicle, and theft. Catherine took the time, while in jail, to decide it was time to get away from David and start over. David had to serve a long jail sentence, while Catherine got off with probation. With the help of her parole officer, she found a job as a housekeeper working for the McLaughlin family. She ended up marrying the families' oldest son, Donald McLaughlin, on her twenty first birthday. They went on to have seven children. One of her children, however, was killed in a car accident while he was only an infant, leaving her with six of her children to take care of. Catherine was never really interested in motherhood though, and wasn't proud of her children and her family like another mother might be. She wasn't concerned about the children or keeping up with the house. Catherine was never truly happy. Her thoughts kept going back to her childhood love, David Birnie. The family that she had left never saw Catherine as a violent or evil person. Not unless she was around David.

Catherine finally reconnected with David Birnie after a thirteen year separation, four weeks after she gave birth to their seventh child. David had escaped from prison and the two of them had begun seeing each other. Catherine left her family and everything behind when David popped back into her life. They finally moved in together and Catherine had her last name changed to Birnie, although the couple never formally or legally got married. They moved into a white brick, two bedroom bungalow on Moorhouse Street. The house was unkempt, the property looked untended, and the house needed a fresh coat of paint. Catherine was completely dependent on David, emotionally and physically. Catherine was easily controlled and manipulated by David, and she would do anything and everything to make him happy. She never wanted to disappoint him. David had an insatiable sexual appetite and was said to have sex up to six times a day. He also accrued an extensive pornography collection and his brother claimed he always had someone. He always had a woman around. David's brother, James, had ended up staying with Catherine and David for a short while. James had just recently been released from prison after serving time for his own sex related offenses. He stayed with the couple for about six months. His brother went on to describe the numbing spray that David would spray on his penis before he had sex with all of the different women.

David and Catherine had exhausted all of their options sexually and began looking for new ways to pleasure themselves. They had spoken about abduction and rape, but had not realized that it would bc just a few short weeks before they turned their fantasies into a heinous and perverted reality. Being as emotionally dependent on David as she was, it was easy for David to talk her into his abduction and rape plans. Catherine could never tell him no. She felt that she couldn't survive without him and would do anything to keep him. Catherine was completely codependent and David always seemed to be in control. She wanted David to have all the pleasure and excitement that he wanted but knew that they had exhausted all efforts between just the two of them.

The abductions, rapes, and brutal murders began on October 6th, 1986. The couple didn't really care who their victims were, as long as they were female and alone. Twenty two year old Mary Neilson arrived at the Moorhouse Street residence to inquire about some tires that David had for sale. Mary was a student at the University of Western Australia where she was pursuing her degree in Psychology. Once inside the house, David took Mary by knife point and chained her to their bed and gagged her. Catherine stood in the room and watched as David raped the girl repeatedly. After the rape, the couple took Mary to Gleneagles National Park. David raped her one more time and then strangled her with a nylon cord and stabbed her through the heart. The couple then buried Mary in a shallow grave. Catherine looked on while David committed these violent acts, however, she did not yet participate.

The second murder took place on October 20th. The victim was fifteen year old, Susannah Candy. Susannah was a high school student attending Hollywood High School. She lived with her parents and had two brothers and one sister. Catherine and David Birnie had been driving around for several hours that night in search of their next victim. The couple finally found a girl walking along Stirling Highway, by herself, trying to hitch a ride. As soon as she got into David's car she had a knife to her throat and she was taken to the Birnies' home. While at the home, she was forced to write letters to her family explaining that she decided to run away. David repeatedly raped Susannah while she lay bound and gagged. Catherine had gotten into the bed with them and tried to strangle her with the nylon cord, but Susannah began fighting back. They forced sleeping pills down her throat, and once she passed out they successfully strangled her with the cord. The couple took Susannah to the State Park and buried her in a shallow grave, like their previous victims. This was the first time that Catherine took part in the murder. Catherine never showed any form of remorse over what she had done. When later asked why she contributed she said, "I wanted to see how strong I was within my inner self. I didn't feel a thing. It was like I expected. I was prepared to follow him to the end of the earth and do anything to see that his desires were satisfied. She was a female. Females hurt and destroy males."

On November 1st, the Killer Couple comes across their third victim, Noelene Patterson. Noelene was on her way home from work when her car ran out of gas. Noelene was a bar manager and had been working at Nedland's Golf Club that day. She was standing beside her car when David pulled up to her and offered his help. The thirty one year old got into David's car and was immediately met with a knife at her throat. She was taken to Moorhouse Street where she was bound and gagged, while being raped repeatedly. The original plan, like the others, was to kill the girl that same night. David had seemed to develop feelings for Noelene however. Catherine noticed the fondness that David had for the woman and became extremely jealous and increasingly upset. Noelene represented the type of person that Catherine could only wish to be and she absolutely despised her because of this. Catherine gave David an ultimatum at this point. She put the knife to her own chest and said, 'you either kill her tonight, or I will kill myself.' It was on the third night, after being given the ultimatum, that David gave Noelene several sleeping pills and then strangled her. She was then taken to the park and buried beside the other victims. Catherine admitted to taking pleasure in throwing sand in the victims face as David coldly buried her with no remorse.

Catherine and David's fourth victim, Denise Brown, suffered the same fate as the previous women who had the unfortunate experience of crossing paths with the Killer Couple. Denise Brown was twenty one years old, and was taken on November 5, 1986 while waiting at a bus stop. She was gagged and raped repeatedly before being put into the car and taken to Pine Plantation, where she was raped again while David waited for a blanket of darkness to fall. After it got dark he took her out and raped her again, while stabbing her in the neck. As David began burying her, thinking she was dead, Denise surprised the couple by sitting straight up in her grave. David struck her in the head twice with an axe as Catherine looked on in shock and amazement. David has said that he learned bodies would decompose at a faster rate if you stabbed them.

Detective Sergeant Paul Ferguson was the first to realize that he could be dealing with a serial killer, after the fourth woman was reported missing. Years later he recalled his experience while working on the case. He recalls how this case still haunts him and when asked why replied, "Because it was the most interesting and horrific I've had in my career," and "I have things tucked away back here that I pray to God I never pull out of the drawer." All of the missing women had come from relatively good homes and they never got into any real trouble. Their families found the phone calls and letters they received very suspicious.

The couples' fifth and final victim was seventeen year old Kate Moir. She was on her way home, after a night out with her friends, when she was abducted by the couple. The date of this final abduction was November 10th, 1986. Kate was the only one of their victims that was able to escape and run and find help. David had left the house for work that day. Catherine was home with Kate. She forced her to call her parents and tell them that she would be staying at a friend's house. When Catherine heard a knock at the door, she left Kate alone, untied, and went to see who was there. Kate took the opportunity to escape through the open window and ran half naked to the nearest store. She ran in crying and pleading for help. Kate was taken to the Palmyra police station and questioned. She was able to give the police a full description of Catherine and David, as well as inform the police of the couples' address. After their arrest, Catherine admitted to knowing Kate, but the couple said that the sexual acts were consensual and she was a willing participant. The police performed a search of the Birnie's home and found Kate's bag, as well as a pack of cigarettes that Kate had managed to hide in the ceiling in order to prove that she was there. After hours of questioning, Catherine and David finally admitted to the rape and murders of the four women and agreed to show the police where they had buried them. Three of the victims had been buried in Gleneagle State Forest and one on the Pine Plantation. The couple showed no emotion, whatsoever, as the police dug up the graves. David was the one who showed the police the locations of the women, except for one. Catherine insisted that she be the one to show them where Noelene was buried. She showed no regret, only anger. She spat on Noelene's grave and made her strong feelings of hate toward her very vocal to the detective. She explained to the police, in great detail, how much she despised Noelene Patterson. As they were leaving, David turned to Detective Katich and said chillingly, "What a pointless loss of young life." They showed absolutely no remorse for what they had done. This statement stuck with the detectives for years to follow. They couldn't believe how little the couple seemed to care or regret what they had been done. In some ways, however, they thought Catherine was relieved that it was finally over.

Catherine admitted to not caring about participating in the rapes and murders of the women, until they got to Denise Brown. "I think I must have come to a decision that sooner or later there had to be an end to the rampage. I had reached the stage when I didn't know what to do. I suppose I came to a decision that I was prepared to give her a chance." The brutal manner in which Denise was murdered seemed to hit Catherine hard. She witnessed David not only stab her repeatedly but strike her in the head with the axe. "Deep and dark in the back of my mind was yet another fear. I had a great fear that I would have to look at another killing like that of Denise Brown, the girl he murdered with the axe."

In response to Kate Moir's escape, due to Catherine's carelessness with her victim, she said, "I knew that it was a foregone conclusion that David would kill her, and probably do it that night. I was just fed up with the killings.

I thought if something did not happen soon it would simply go on and on and never end."

Kate Moir survived the abduction and attacks of Australia's most infamous serial killers. Instead of remaining a victim, she chose to be a survivor. She also sought to seek reform for the way her government handled cases like hers.

"I want to see no parole for wilful murder. I want a reintroduction of wilful murder as a charge. I want truth in sentencing. I want no parole for sex offenders and child sex offenders. We have been softening our justice system for years."

Kate Moir is a married woman and mother of three children. She constantly fights for the changes and justice she deserves. The following are quotes that were made by Kate, again concerning Catherine's parole and the possibility of her release.

"I want the legacy that I leave to be that of a survivor and a hero, not a victim. But enough is enough."

"I want the Attorney General to change the law and stop reviewing Catherine Birnie's parole. She does not apply for it herself, it is automatically reviewed and every time it happens, it causes me incredible pain."

"Every time I hear that her parole is being reviewed, I relive the nightmare. It causes significant trauma because I relive it and it feels like it happened yesterday. My name was always protected because I was a minor at the time I was captured, but due to the internet, if anybody googles my name it is everywhere and linked to the Birnie killings."

The couple appeared in court on November 12th, 1986. This was just two days after their fifth victim had escaped and they were arrested. The court proceedings took place at Fremantle Magistrates Court. They both refused any kind of representation, no plea was entered, bail was refused, and they were remanded into custody. Catherine allegedly took photos and the couple also recorded video of their criminal acts. At trial, the police were in possession of the video evidence. On February 10, 1987 a crowd gathered outside of the courthouse. When they saw the couple being ushered in for trial they screamed and chanted, "Hang the Bastards!" The community was outraged over the news of the serial killings that took place and wanted David and Catherine to receive the maximum sentence. They even wanted to reinstate the death penalty for David and Catherine Birnie.

Bill Power, the court reporter, spoke about the proceedings and the manners in which the couple acted while in court. He said that it would be something that would always stick with him, he would never forget.

"There was nothing distinctive about David and Catherine when they first appeared in court to face multiple murder charges in the serial killings which brought an end to the mystery of young women going missing off Perth streets."

"They were a rather nondescript, ordinary looking couple you might find running a petrol station in a country town. David was a weedy little man and Catherine his drab, slightly buxom wife with a very sour face. Both were accompanied by male police officers."

"If you have ever witnessed a wild cat go off, then try and imagine some hellcat in the confined spaces of a narrow staircase. Catherine Birnie fought against the guarding police officers and refused to allow any of them to touch her as she screamed and spat her words at them until she reached the dock and spotted her beloved, David. Only then did she calm down."

It had also been said previously, by some people in the community that the couple never looked like the type that could commit such violent acts. They looked like normal and ordinary people. But the secret horrors of what occurred in their home on Moorhouse Street would paint a very different image of the couple.

Trial Judge Justice Wallace said in trial, "Each of these horrible crimes were premeditated, planned, and carried out cruelly and relentlessly over a comparatively short period."

Right before Judge Wallace sentenced Catherine, he delivered the following message to her. He explained that he did not believe that even though she pled guilty, that she was truly sorry for what she had done. She had pled guilty and avoided a long trial, and spared the victims' families from having to relive over and over what happened to their loved ones, but she showed no remorse, no emotion, no sympathy for the crimes she had committed with David Birnie.

"You willingly joined in the selection of your unfortunate victims, carried them off at knifepoint, and held them in captivity for the sole purpose of the sexual gratification of your partner in crime and then murdered them, lest you be identified, and then finally mutilated them. You personally extinguished the life of two of your victims and certainly participated in the death of the third. The only appropriate punishment is the sentence I intend to impose, strict life security in prison."

Remember, Catherine was completely devoted, obsessed, and brainwashed when it came to David. She would do anything and everything for him to make sure he was happy. This is the driving factor that David used to manipulate and control her. He needed an accomplice and she was more than willing, and he knew it. Catherine and David received four separate life sentences for the abduction, torture, rape, and murder of Mary Neilson, Susannah Candy, Noelene Patterson, and Denise Brown. Under sentencing laws, their case was brought up every three years automatically for parole. Kate began a crusade to ensure that the couple remained in prison. She grew a social media presence and page entitled, We Support Kate, as well as worked with the Empowerment Foundation in an attempt to build an online reform petition. Kate also received support from Catherine's son, Peter. He chose not to release his surname to the public, due to the physical and emotional abuse he has been forced to face in relation to his mother's crimes. He had suffered personal and professional ruin, as soon as people learned about his family history. He had been turned down for jobs, lost jobs he had, and even lost his fiancé because of his family background. Peter was only five years old when his mother was arrested. He saw his mother on television because of it shortly after her arrest. When speaking out on the abuse he faced, he recalled horrible stories of what happened to him, and his siblings, while growing up. He also stated that the mandatory parole hearings, every three years, prevented him from getting on with his life. Having to hear about his mother and relive the violence his mother was responsible for every few years, was an interruption to his life, and it made it harder to maintain a sense of normalcy within his career life and personal life. In an interview with the West Australian, Peter stated, "I want the parole board to hear I don't want her out. I don't want to see her out." He also said, "I have had baseball bats to the head, I have been jumped on and kicked at. I have been knocked out."

After pleading guilty and receiving their sentences, David was initially sent to maximum security Fremantle Prison, he was eventually moved into solitary confinement. He did not get along with the other prisoners and was constantly getting into fights. The inmates frequently and violently attacked David. A day before he was due in trial for the charge of rape of an inmate, David hung himself in his jail cell. His suicide occurred in 2009 at Casuarina Prison. Catherine's request to attend David's funeral was refused.

Catherine was sent to Bandyup Women's prison where she was eventually employed as the head librarian. While in prison, the couple exchanged over 2600 letters, but were denied any other form of contact. Catherine's mandatory parole hearings were finally revoked in 2009, and her papers were subsequently marked: 'never to be released.'

While many people are against Catherine Birnie ever getting parole, one man stands against this argument. Perth QC Tom Percy disagrees with the opinion of people that had been saying that some people just don't deserve a second chance. The following quotes by Percy outline his argument of Catherine not remaining in prison and the likelihood of her harming the community, as well as his stance of being in favor of Catherine's parole.

"She should not be kept in prison to satisfy society's thirst for revenge."

"She has been there thirty odd years and you would think it might be time for us to say she has done her time. She has done her statutory minimum prescribed by the court, which was in possession of all of the facts."

"I am not sure she could really be a threat to anyone anymore, and all my information from Bandyup Womens' Prison is that she is a little old granny that goes about her work in the library like a church mouse."

"This case just so happened to be one that caught the public attention, even though she was not the prime mover in it. David is now dead."

"What's the point of keeping her in there? Sadly, it looks like she will never get parole, but I think she probably deserves it."

Despite his argument and fight to get Catherine released from prison, she still remains behind bars. She has not requested any new parole hearings, herself, as of yet. Some people in the community had gone as far as to say that if she were to be released, then maybe Percy should allow her to live with him in his residence.

It was now January of 1987. A letter written by Catherine Birnie, while in prison, eventually surfaced. It was a letter she had written to her six children in an attempt to explain some of her actions that led to her being placed in prison and why she left them in the first place. The letter reads as followed:

"Dear kids, Hi! Mum here...the reason I changed my name to Birnie was so that you kids wouldn't be hurt by the newspapers and television people. I am not proud of what has been said about me, but I have to live with that and the memories. As to why this happened, I can only hope that the doctors can help me to find out.....I never stopped loving any of you kids. Maybe I was wrong about leaving you but I thought you would be safer with your father."

Catherine's husband, Donald, claimed that he had still wanted her back. This was after trial and after he heard of the horrific acts she had committed with David. He stated, 'you can't stop loving someone after fifteen years of marriage.' Donald's mother stood firmly beside her son, saying that Catherine had been good and non-violent, until David cast his spell over her. Catherine's nephew, Leonard Nock, stood beside his aunt claiming, "All Aunt Cathy wanted was someone to lean on. She never had a mother. She is a very caring person. She and I are very close. I used to call her my mum. She was never the violent type, she never used to hit the kids. It is not the Cathy we used to know and love." In Catherine's letter she also persuaded the children to tell their father to divorce her. She said their father needed to move on and this was the way it needed to be done. She didn't hold out any hope for her eventual release and didn't want Donald to wait for her, because it was never going to happen. She also asked the children to get permission from Donald to write back to her, and maybe even one day go and visit her. The family put the entirety of the blame on David. They refused to admit to or believe that Catherine had anything to do with the violence. During their prison visits, the family also failed to even ask Catherine the question regarding her guilt or innocence. They didn't want to hear the answer, therefore, they never even asked the question.

Catherine Bernie was up for parole in 2013 and again in 2016. She was denied both years. She is once again up for review sometime in 2019. "Now barring any reason to keep her in, and revenge I don't consider enough of a reason. She should be released."-Percy

Despite Percy's statements, Catherine Birnie remains in prison to this very day, with little to no chance of parole. People, even to this day, wonder if the abductions, the perverse rape, and heinous murders would have continued long past the few weeks they had gotten away with it. If they had never been caught, would they have continued? Finally, were there other victims that they never confessed to? Other gravesites that have yet to be located? It is too late for David Birnie to tell anyone, but Catherine still has the chance to admit to any other wrongdoing she had done before her permanent home in prison forced her to keep distance between herself and her lover. I guess we will never know.

"I honestly believe that woman has never given those victims one ounce of consideration, both the dead victims and the families of the victims...They [David and Catherine Birnie] were parasites who lived off of each other. The most evil people I have ever, ever come across."-Detective Paul Ferguson.

BABY KILLER

The True Story of Amelia Dyer

Chrissy Eubank

Amelia Dyer, considered one of the most prolific serial killers in history, was born around 1837 in Victorian Britain. Her picture on the front cover easily betrays the evil that resided within her heart. Her reign of terror lasted over twenty years, as she is projected to have killed as many as 400 children before finally being caught

She embarked on a thirty year career of killing with eyewitnesses seeing at least six babies entering her house a day. The count of 400 dead is a conservative estimate.

EARLY LIFE

Amelia was the youngest of five children born into the tiny town of Pyle Marsh. She had three older brothers, Thomas, James, and William along with an older sister named Ann. Her father was a shoemaker named Samuel Hobley and her mother was named Sarah Weymouth.

But he didn't come from an impoverished family like so many others during the Victorian Era.

"For the time, she had a pretty good start," said author Allison Rattle. "Her father had a pretty good trade and paid for her to go to church and school which at the time only a quarter of the children her age actually got an education so she was privileged in that respect."

She found entertainment in reading and used to write poetry herself. Amelia's mother Sarah, however, became mentally ill after suffering from typhus fever. Amelia had to suffer through watching her mother's seizures and outbursts, providing care for her until she died in 1848.

"She witnessed her mother basically losing her mind," said Rattle. "And dying a slow, horrific death. I guess being a young girl she may have been called upon to nurse her mother slightly or at least wait upon her."

Psychologists have posited that it was going through this trauma of watching her mother lose her mind, that caused Amelia's own emotional wiring to run askew.

"Amelia would later claim that her mother died as a result of hereditary insanity," said author Allison Vale. "I think though that this isn't true but it's really easy to understand how she could have remembered it that way."

"It was certain to have a massive impact on her and she may have learned a few things about what kind of symptoms might be shown by someone whose losing their mind."

Amelia was sent to live with her aunt in nearby Bristol after her mother's death. She started an apprenticeship with a corset maker and worked there until her father died in 1859. The oldest brother, Thomas, took control of the family shoe business. Two years later, some type of estrangement occurred with her brothers, specifically James and Amelia doesn't appear to have further ties with her family.

In 1861, Amelia moved to Trinity Street, Bristol. She married George Thomas, who at 59 years old was 35 years Amelia's senior. The two lied about their ages on their marriage certificate with George claiming he was 48 years old and Amelia claiming she was 30.

A CAREER IN "HEALTH CARE"

Amelia began training as a nurse after she got married.

"Amelia turned to one of the most arduous professions she could have turned to," Vale said. "Nursing was just starting to change. It was post-Crimean war. Nursing was starting to have a much better profile as a result of Florence Nightingale. But it was still a thankless profession."

"It wasn't a caring profession like it is present day," agreed psychologist Laura Richards. "They train you psychologically to be a lot more robust around dealing with people. So she became quite hardy and emotionless from having been trained through the nursing regime."

Amelia became pregnant at the age of twenty-six before she met a woman named Ellen Dane who came to boarder at her house. Dane was a midwife who told her of a lucrative and shady way to earn money. Amelia would use her own home as a front to provide housing for women who had gotten pregnant out of wedlock. They would them give the babies away for adoption or kill them through malnutrition.

They called it baby farming.

"Amelia could see it was a very easy way to make money," Rattle said. "Although with risks involved obviously although Amelia did have training as a mid-wife as well through her nursing experience so it was certainly something she knew she was capable of doing. That was the beginning of a massive change in Amelia's life."

Dane moved her base of operations to the USA while Amelia took her "business plan" to heart. During this time, unmarried mothers did not have access to any kind of subsidy as the 1834 Poor Law Amendment Act did not oblige the fathers of illegitimate children to pay for their upbringing. These laws, coupled with the stigmatization of single mothers, forced the practice of baby farming.

Amelia discussed business strategies with Dane. She knew the best bet was to insist on being paid upfront with a one-time fee. She refused any type of money for continuous care as she knew that would mean the mother would return to visit.

"The one off premiums were certainly not enough to sustain a child's life for long financially," Vale said. "And the only way that it would be profitable for a baby farmer was to subject a child to persist underfeeding that would at some point bring about the infant's death."

"Abortion was not an option," Judith Knelman said. "So the simplest thing to do was hide, have the baby and get rid of it. Pay somebody to take care of it or pay somebody to get rid of it."

The babies were subsequently left on the premises and seen as "nurse children."

"Illegitimacy was seen as hugely immoral," said author Allison Rattle. "Even orphanages would only accept orphans from families where the parents were married and the father had died. They wouldn't accept a child who was born out of wedlock."

"Dickens did a really good job of describing social conditions in the 1850 and 60s," Knelman added. "Certainly there were a lot of poor people. There were a lot of neglected and abandoned children."

"There was no work," said Alan McCormick of Scotland Yard. "There was no social services. There was no welfare. One in every twelve women was a prostitute. A child being born in normal circumstances only had a fifty percent chance of reaching the age of five. So that's how bad it was."

BABY FARMING

"Baby farming was a business carried out throughout the country," said historian Ken Wells. "If a mother was unable to look after their child, there was an option of sending them out to a baby farmer, also known as fostering, with the understanding that they could visit the child whenever they wanted to."

On the surface they were providing a service to a growing need. They took an unwanted child and gave them to a foster parent. Only those foster parents and caregivers didn't always have the best interests of the infant at heart.

"MOTHER'S FRIEND"

The majority of these "caregivers" resorted to starving out the babies. They sedated crying babies with alcohol or drugs usually using Godfrey's Cordial, also known as 'Mother's Friend'. This syrup was one of the most popular medicines given to infants and children in both the United States and England in the latter years of the 18th and early 19th centuries. The syrup was used as a panacea to everything from colic to jaundice to excessive crying to diarrhea. 'Mother's Friend' was harmful despite its harmless sounding name as it contained one grain of opium for every two ounces. Many infants were poisoned from this syrup which was administered in secret by nurses who wanted to keep babies under their care in a deep state of sleep and thus more manageable.

"A hungry child, a noisy child, is a difficult child to raise," author Allison Vale said. "And something that was chillingly referred to colloquially as 'the Quietness' was an over the counter anti-colic cordial and it did contain liquid opium which was laudanum and in some cases brandy."

"People gave babies laudanum when they were supposed to be giving them food," Klansman said. "Because it dulled the need, or dulled the awareness of the baby that it was hungry. Of course it didn't nourish the baby so eventually a baby that was given that and not given enough food would die."

The babies would die from severe malnutrition but the coroner would record the death as "debility from birth", "lack of breast milk" or "starvation."

There were those guilt-ridden mothers who returned to the baby-farming homes to check on their children but would find their efforts blocked. Most would be too scared or embarrassed to inform the police of any wrongdoing. The police themselves had numerous problems tracking any children that were deemed missing.

"Dead infants," Vale said. "Or abandoned infants were as commonplace in British cities as roadkill today. Babies were found parceled up in railroad stations, under railroad arches."

"It was desperation," McCormick added. "For the vast majority of these ladies."

TO A MANNER BORN

With Dane's departure to the States, Amelia set her sights on taking her place in the baby-farming business. She had just given birth to her own daughter, Ellen, but in 1869 her husband George died.

A widow at age 32 with a baby, Amelia needed a new source of income...

She began taking in pregnant women as she placed ads to nurse and adopt the babies. In return, she required a large one-time fee and clothing for the child. She began meeting with expectant young women, convincing them that she was someone who could be trusted in providing a safe and loving home for their child.

Before she followed through with her plan, however, she put her own child up for adoption and sent her away.

"It was a choice that she made," Vale said. "She had options. She could have worked through. But instead what she does is to farm her own child out and opt for the easy money that she seemed to be able to make."

"As Amelia chose to go into the baby farming business," Rattle said. "She was maybe able to travel around here, there and everywhere adopting babies so it made sense for her daughter to be out of the way."

Three years after her first husband George died, Amelia remarried. His name was William Dyer, a brewers laborer from Bristol. They had two children together, Mary Ann aka Polly and William Samuel.

Amelia eventually left William, however, as the latter lost his job and offered little in the way of finances.

Strapped for cash, Amelia decided to dispense with the heavy cost of letting the babies die through neglect and starvation. So after each child was born she promptly murdered them, thus incurring a windfall of profits.

"Baby farmers used different methods," Klansman said. "Some of which are less palatable than others."

"Quite often she would suffocate babies at birth," Rattle said. "Smothering the baby the moment its head came out, before it turned blue as that would be a sign that it had taken its first breath. (She made) it would look like a stillbirth so the death certificate would all be above board."

When her daughter Polly asked why so many babies came and disappeared, Amelia described herself as the "angel maker."

"I'm sending little children to Jesus," Amelia said. "Because he wanted them far more than their mothers did."

"Cold," Alan McCormick of New Scotland Yard said in describing Amelia. "Those kids meant nothing to her. It was just a means of getting money."

It can be argued, however, that once Amelia got a taste of killing she did it more for the power than the money and greed.

"The actual killing of the child," Holmes said. "Watching the child peacefully to some degree die. It parallels perhaps seeing her mother pass away where she felt an almost God-like power over these children that she had decided were going to go to their maker."

AROUSING SUSPICION

"Amelia was already aware of the fact that this was not going to be about her helping children," forensic psychologist David Holmes said. "This was going to be a fairly cruel and anti-mothering act that would be carried out in order to gain all of this money."

Amelia successfully avoided police involvement until 1879, a good ten years into her murderous ways. A doctor became suspicious about the number of child deaths he had been called in to certify under Amelia's care.

"The inquests were held in Somerset," Vale said. "And they're (the police) pretty certain that the babies have died as a direct result of neglect and opium overdose. But they can't prove it. And interestingly, she gets off with a six months sentence with hard labor."

Without a coroner that was able to rule completely against her, Amelia would have undoubtedly been executed by hanging.

"Its incredibly really," Rattle said. "That she only got six months. And there was one example, we read of a chap who got twelve months for stealing a piece of bacon."

Amelia took the punishment hard, becoming an emotional wreck during her jail stay. She resumed her business, however, as soon as she was released.

"In the long term," Holmes reasoned. "It mostly would have served as a very hard lesson in forensic awareness that she wasn't gonna get caught again. And there was no way she was going to leave any evidence which had been the problem in leading up to her capture."

She was sent to mental hospitals for supposed mental illness and suicidal ideations but these seemed to be well-timed acts. From her experience of working in an asylum, Amelia knew the tricks of the trade in order to make her stay an easy one.

"I don't think Amelia Dyer was insane," said Vale. "I think she was a very bad person who deliberately committed murder for profit."

Amelia had both an alcohol and substance abuse problem, using on a regular basis as she began her killings once again.

"Certainly the drugs would have had an impact on her," Richards said. "On her mental state. Maybe induced this complete detachment from reality."

"A long term laudanum habit," Vale concurred. "Will lead to periods of depression. It can lead to mood swings even when you're not under the influence. I think it also exacerbates any underlying mental health issues."

RETURNING TO BABY FARMING

In 1884, British society took a much harder line against baby farming and any sign of neglect or abuse would be reported.

"She definitely changes her modus operandi at this point (after 1884)," Vale said. "She's beginning to murder these children."

In 1890, Amelia took on the care of the illegitimate baby of a governess. She had begun targeting the babies of the more affluent because of the larger amounts of money involved. The higher up the social class the woman was, however, the more risk was involved as the woman may have means to question and come after Amelia.

"This was a young governess who fell in love with the young master of the house that she worked in and had got pregnant," Rattle said. "She was left on her own and she responds to an advert, gets in touch with Amelia Dyer and moves in with her. Amelia was able to gain the trust of this woman as with many others, so much so that the governess was persuaded to leave her baby in the care of Amelia once it was born."

The governess, however, returned to visit her baby months later and immediately became suspicious that the child she was given was not hers. She stripped the baby to see if a birth mark was present on one of its hips. It wasn't and the governess immediately informed the authorities.

The police, however, could never pin Amelia down.

"She managed to put them off time and time again by sending them on wild goose chases," Rattle said. "She said she had sent them to a couple that moved here...that moved there."

Amelia continued to move from town to town but still found herself being stalked by the governess who wouldn't give up.

"She did feel hounded," Richards said. "I'm sure that would have had an impact on her. She would have felt that pressure."

Amelia then feigned another nervous breakdown and a doctor was brought in. "The birds are telling me to do it! The birds are telling me to do it!" she would cry out, forcing the doctor to send her to an asylum.

"She was a very clever lady," Holmes said. "With the police getting close to her and she needed to lose herself and what better place to go than somewhere like that (a mental asylum)."

Her mental illness continued on unabated as she drank two bottles of laudanum in an attempted suicide. Her long term use of opium, however, allowed her to build up the tolerance necessary to survive.

"Amelia would be drawn to the idea of self-medicating," Holmes said. "Possibly seeing it as a route, a means to ease the situation, make it even easier for her to put up with what she was doing."

"She took it (opium) on a regular basis," Richards said. "She took it almost daily so she was an addict. So that would induce a form of state from her mentally where she would be detached from reality and I think that was part of her coping mechanism to detach from the reality of what she was doing."

After that close call and subsequent hospital release, Amelia resumed baby farming and murder.

"Her mental breakdowns were very short lived," Richards noted. "She would be out of sorts for a period of time that get it all back together again. To me that would say there isn't a mental illness there."

A CLEVER KILLER

She wised up to doing things on the books and decided to stop getting doctors to issue death certificates. Amelia decided to kill and bury the bodies herself. In order to do this, she would have to be a killer on the run as inevitably the mothers would come back seeking to reclaim their children or check on their welfare. Amelia took her family to different cities to escape suspicion as soon as things got too hot. She would use a series of different aliases and rename her businesses.

"Amelia committed what many serial killers do," Holmes explained. "The mistake of accelerating and being over enthusiastic. Either for reasons that she was enjoying the process or quite simply greed was driving her over the edge."

Baby farming began to gain the attention and compassion of the British ruling class, however. They asked why if they had laws for the prevention of the cruelty of animals then why didn't there laws protecting children. With the arrest and hanging of Margaret Waters (another baby farming killer) and the fleeing Dyer, Amelia's colleagues were going downhill fast and perhaps she thought her time was limited.

By 1893, Amelia had another breakdown but was released from the Wells mental asylum. This would be the last time she would be hospitalized. She moved to

Caversham, Berkshire with a woman named Jane "Granny" Smith who didn't know of Amelia's exploits.

"She befriends an old lady named Jane Smith," Vale said. "She's widowed and resigned to spend her last days in the workhouse. Amelia seduces her with stories of rescuing the unwanted infants. Of nursing them. And it's a very, very seductive image. And Jane Smith buys into it, wholesale."

Her daughter Mary Ann aka Polly and her husband Arthur Palmer came along as well.

The group moved to 45 Kensington Road, Reading Berkshire in that same year. Amelia had the perfect front. She coached Jane Smith to call her "mother" in front of prospective clients while Amelia would call her "Granny."

A ruse to project a mother-daughter image and put the guards down of the pregnant young women.

"Jane Smith didn't get the life she was promised at all," Rattle said. "She was treated as no more than a servant really. She was made to look after the children, to clean the house."

Amelia then puts her adoptions into overdrive. The babies come in and out of the house with such rapidity that old lady Jane Smith doesn't even learn their names.

Eyewitnesses later claimed that there were six infants a day coming to and from the house daily.

THE MURDERS CONTINUE

The advertisement in the "Miscellaneous" column of the Bristol Times & Mirror newspaper was poignant.

In January of 1896 a popular barmaid named Evelina Marmon gave birth to a daughter out of wedlock. She named the baby Doris and she sought immediately to have it adopted. She placed an ad in the "Miscellaneous" section of the Bristol Times & Mirror newspaper.

"Wanted, respectable woman to take young child." Marmon intended to go back to work and hoped to eventually reclaim her child.

Evelina was a God-fearing farmer's daughter who left the farm for city life. She found work as a barmaid in the saloon of the Plough Hotel, an old coaching inn. She was buxom with blonde hair and had a vibrant personality. She had plenty of suitors and became pregnant by one of the male patrons who left her deserted.

Evelina knew she could not bring up the baby on her own.

She would have to find a foster home for little Doris - to have her "adopted out", in the language of the time - go back to work and hope in time to be able to reclaim her child.

Next to her own ad was an advertisement that read *"Married couple with no family would adopt healthy child, nice country home. Terms, £10".*

Marmon answered the ad which was addressed to a "Mrs. Harding", an alias of Amelia. A few days later Amelia wrote back, saying *"I should be glad to have a dear little baby girl, one I could bring up and call my own. We are plain, homely people, in fairly good circumstances. I don't want a child for money's sake, but for company and home comfort... Myself and my husband are dearly fond of children. I have no child of my own. A child with me will have a good home and a mother's love. It is just lovely here, heatlhy and pleasant. There is an orchard opposite our front door."*

Evelina was assured that she could visit whenever she wished.

"Rest assured I will do my duty by that dear child. I will be a mother, as far as lies in my power."

"It is just lovely here, healthy and pleasant. There is an orchard opposite our front door."

Evelina tried to negotiate a weekly fee for the care of Doris but Amelia wanted a substantial one-time fee to be paid upfront. Evelina, seemingly with no other choice, agreed to pay the £10, and a week later "Mrs Harding" arrived in Cheltenham.

Evelina was surprised that Amelia aka "Mrs. Harding" was old (59 years) and heavy set (over 210 lbs). She remained reluctant at first but gave in as the elderly woman immediately showed her Doris some affection, covering her with a shawl.

Evelina gave the old lady a cardboard box of clothes she had prepared – nappies, chemises, petticoats, frocks, nightgowns, and a powder box. She also enclosed the money and received a signed receipt from "Mrs.Harding."

She accompanied her baby daughter and her eventual killer to Cheltenham station then on to Gloucester. Evelina stood there crying through the hot steam on the platform as the 5:20 p.m train took her baby away.

When Evelina returned home, she described herself as "a broken woman."

Days later, she received a letter from "Mrs. Harding" offering her assurance that all was well with her daughter. Evelina wrote back but received no replies afterward.

Amelia told Evelina that she would be going to Reading but lied. She traveled to 76 Mayo Road, Willesden, London where her daughter Mary Ann was staying. Amelia then took some white edging tape and wrapped it around the baby's neck, making a strangling knot. The baby did not die immediately.

"I used to like to watch them with the tape around their neck," Amanda said. "But it was soon all over with them."

"The idea of strangling and using the tape may make it seem almost symbolical or bizarre to ourselves," Holmes said. "But in terms of criminal awareness she was aware of the fact that if she tried to suffocate a baby its not always absolutely certain that the baby is dead."

The mother and daughter team wrapped the baby up with a napkin. They kept the clothes that Evelina gave her and hoped to sell it to a pawnbroker. Amelia used some of the money to pay the rent to her landlady and gave the woman a pair of child's boots as a present for her own little girl.

The following day, April 1st of 1896, a young boy named Harry Simmons was taken to the Mayo Road residence. Amelia had no spare white edging tape available and used the tape from Doris' corpse to strangle the year old boy.

The next day both bodies were rolled into a carpet bag, their corpses stacked one on top of the other. Bricks were added inside for additional weight. Amelia headed back toward Reading, taking the bus to Paddington and then the train. She dragged the carpet bag through the streets until she reached the River Thames. She had a secluded spot at Caversham Lock and she forced the carpet bag through the railing and didn't leave until she heard it splash into the waters below.

She didn't know she had a witness as a man passed, hurrying on his way home calling out "Good night."

A SHOCKING DISCOVERY

Ironically, only days before the dumping of the bodies a package was fished out of the Thames by a bargeman. This package was the work of Amelia as she had not weighed it down adequately. It contained the body of a baby girl named Helena Fry. With only a small police force available in Reading, a Constable Anderson made a significant discovery. He found a label from Temple Meads Station, Bristol and he used microscopic analysis of the wrapping paper. He found a faintly legible name. A "Mrs.Thomas" and an address.

The address of Amelia Dyer.

The police immediately placed Amelia's home under surveillance. They did enough research on Amelia and knew that she would "disappear" if she thought she was under suspicion. So they decided they would be better served if they would use a young woman as a decoy to secure a meeting with Amelia and discuss the prospect of using her "adoptive services."

On April 3rd, while Amelia was waiting on the decoy to arrive, she answered the door to a police raid. The smell of decomposing bodies radiated throughout her home but no human remains were found. The police found other evidence, however, such as the white edging tape, telegrams describing adoption arrangements, pawn tickets for children's clothing, receipts for newspaper ads and letters from distraught mothers asking about the welfare of their child.

The police determined that in the few months Amelia had been in Reading at least twenty children had been placed into her care. She had been preparing to move again, this time to the town of Somerset.

Amelia was arrested on April 4th, three days after the murders of Doris Marmon and Harry Simmons. The Thames River was searched and six more bodies were discovered, including Doris and Harry.

Each child had been strangled with the seamstress white tape and Amelia later told police that "was how you could tell it was one of mine."

Eleven days later, Evelina Marmon had been contacted by police as they found her name in items found in Amelia's home. Distraught, she came to identify her daughter's remains.

THE TRIAL OF A KILLER

An inquest was held a month later. Amelia's daughter Mary Ann and her husband Arthur were not charged as there was no direct evidence that they were her accomplices. Arthur was set free because of a confession handwritten by Amelia. She wrote:

Sir will you kindly grant me the favour of presenting this to the magistrates on Saturday the 18th instant I have made this statement out, for I may not have the opportunity then I must relieve my mind I do know and I feel my days are numbered on this earth but I do feel it is an awful thing drawing innocent people into trouble I do know I shal have to answer before my Maker in Heaven for the awful crimes I have committed but as God Almighty is my judge in Heaven a on Hearth neither my daughter Mary Ann Palmer nor her husband Alfred Ernest Palmer I do most solemnly declare neither of them had any thing at all to do with it, they never knew I contemplated doing such a wicked thing until it was to late I am speaking the truth and nothing but the truth as I hope to be forgiven, I myself and I alone must stand before my Maker in Heaven to give an answer for it all witnes my hand

Amelia Dyer.

—April 16, 1896

On May 22nd, 1896, Amelia appeared in court and pleaded guilty to the murder of Doris Marmon. Her family and friends testified that they had their own suspicions about Amelia and spoke of times that she evaded discovery. A man came forth claiming he had seen and spoken to Amelia as she had disposed of two bodies at Caversham Lock proved key to the prosecution.

Amelia used insanity as a defense, offering her stays in mental asylums as proof of her instability. The prosecution, however, argued that her symptoms were well-rehearsed actions to avoid suspicion as both of her hospital stays coincided with times that Amelia felt her murders would be discovered.

The jury took four and a half minutes to find her guilty. Amelia then spent three weeks in her condemned cell, filling five journals with her confessions. A chaplain visited her the night before her execution and asked if she had anything to confess. She offered him her journals, asking "isn't this enough?"

Amelia was then subpoenaed to appear as a witness in her daughter's own trial for murder which was set for a week after her own execution date. The court ruled, however, that Amelia became "legally dead" after she was sentenced and her testimony would be inadmissible.

On the day of her execution, Amelia discovered that the charges against her daughter had been dropped.

On June 10th, 1896, Amelia Dyer was hanged by James Billington at Newgate Prison. Asked on the scaffold if she had anything to say, she said "I have nothing to say."

URBAN LEGEND?

It remains unknown as to why Amelia's daughter Mary Ann aka Polly was never convicted. Her own daughter provided the majority of the testimony that procured the conviction of her mother but nothing is said about her own involvement.

And the baby murders did not stop after Amelia's death.

Two years after her execution, railroad workers inspecting carriages found a parcel tied up with a string inside a siding on the Plymouth express.

Inside was a three-week old baby girl. The infant was shivering and wet...but alive.

A little research showed that the baby was the child of a widow named Jane Hill. Hill had given the baby to a woman named "Mrs. Stewart" for the one time fee of £12.

"The little one would have a good home and a parent's love and care," Mrs. Stewart had written, her prose eerilly echoing that of Amelia Dyer. "Mrs. Stewart" had picked up the baby at Plymouth and dumped her on the next train.

The conjecture was that "Mrs. Stewart" was none other than Polly, Amelia's daughter.

SATAN'S DAUGHTER

THE TRUE STORY OF NATASHA CORNETT

TRISH SAMUELSON

Natasha Cornett was born January 26th, 1979 in Pikeville, Kentucky.

Pikeville is located in the foothills of the Appalachian mountains. It is a mining town with most of its inhabitants devoutly religious.

"It's very beautiful scenery to grow up in," Cornett said. "But it's a suffocating place to live."

Born poor, Natasha was the product of an affair between her mother Madonna Wallen and her biological father, a police officer named Roger Burgess.

Her mother then left her husband, Ed Wallen, and raised Natasha alone. They lived in a trailer in Pikeville, Kentucky.

"She had energy to burn," her mother said. "She liked to draw. To read. She liked dogs and babies."

SCHOOL LIFE

Natasha was a good student in elementary school, behaving well and getting good grades. She seemed to be on the right path until one morning she found her mother laying unconscious. Madonna Wallen had overdosed on prescription drugs.

"My momma is on the bed naked," Cornett recalled. "With a bottle of pills laying next to her. I didn't know she was dying. It messed with me."

Around this time, Cornett's life began a downward spiral. She began suffering from anorexia. Then drugs. Then she began engaging in acts of self-mutilation, cutting her arms to "relieve her pain."

"Natasha started to engage in those acts as a means of getting control," forensic psychologist Roberta Nixon said. "She can control her diet. She can control her anger, or so she thinks, by cutting herself. She can control how she feels by doing drugs. Having a dim-witted mother certainly didn't help things either."

At one point, Natasha had lost over thirty pounds because of her anorexia as well as having over seventy cuts on her arms.

"I started cutting because I started going through a rough time with my mom," Natasha said. "It was a release."

"I don't know where that pain comes from," Natasha's mother, Madonna Wallen said. "She just says she has to do it to take away her pain."

In later court testimony, however, Wallen would admit to a history of physical abuse with her daughter.

"I used a belt one time and the buckles slipped from my hand," Wallen said. "And it hit her on the back of the leg. But it made a bruise on her."

Wallen later said that there was sexual abuse of Natasha by her husband whom she originally believed to be Natasha's father.

"Natasha had a really bad upbringing," C. Berkeley Bell, the District Attorney General for Tennessee said. "Lot of hard times. She came from a very dysfunctional family. Hard time in school. Was an outcast. Was ostracized by her classmates."

HIGH SCHOOL DROPOUT

Natasha entered high school but dropped out before her freshman year was complete. Her best friend was Karen Howell who would later be part of the "Wild Bunch" that Cornett would lead on a killing spree.

"Karen was my life raft," Natasha said. "She was the only person that understood me and let me be me. She knew my pain. She went through the same stuff."

Like Natasha, Karen had a dysfunctional family. Her father was an abusive alcoholic and her mother had a nervous breakdown. She came from a strict, religious family with her mother forcing her to stand on a Bible when she misbehaved. She was also bipolar.

"They were like two peas in a pod," Nixon said. "But in court interviews Natasha seems to more of a realization of what took place that night. Karen remained a petulant teenager, sullen and angry. Natasha was the better talker of the two so Karen followed her lead.

BIPOLAR DISORDER

Natasha was eventually diagnosed with bipolar disorder and in one episode had to be hospitalized at the Ridge Treatment Center in

Lexington, KY. She had to leave the hospital after eleven days, however, as that was all the time the state health benefits would allow.

"Bipolar disease is brutal and even more so for people in low income circumstances," Nixon said. "It is extremely hard to treat. The amazing thing here is that she was only hospitalized for eleven days. After that, she doesn't appear to have gone through any kind of outpatient treatment program aside from an aborted session with a counselor. With people like Natasha, they need medication to keep their anxiety and impulses under control. Without it, anything can happen and anything will happen."

Natasha's mother began to see the rapid decline in her emotional state. Her choice of clothing would be reflect her mood and growing anger.

"From the seventh grade," Wallen said. "She just started changing. The big baggy pants. The rope with the emblems hanging. Everybody thought it was weird."

"I started drinking and smoking and associating with people that were weird," Natasha said. "You don't have to be perfect around them."

Natasha sought acceptance and eventually found it in the Goth subculture. Still, with the rapid mood shifts and change in dress, Natasha's own mother insists that there are three versions of Natasha.

"There is the sweet, caring girl," Wallen said. "There is the girl who would do anything for her friends, and there is a dark side that likes to play on a Oujia board, do seances and play vampire games."

MARRIAGE

At the age of seventeen, Natasha married Stephen Cornett. It was no ordinary ceremony, however. The bride and groom wore black and dog collars.

"We'd been friends for awhile," Natasha said. "It seemed like the logical thing to do."

The union only lasted a couple of months. Steven left without warning, abandoning Natasha. The dissolution of the marriage caused Natasha to spiral further into depression.

"It was awful," Natasha said. "I just kinda caved in on myself."

Natasha then fully immersed herself in the Goth subculture even further. She donned black clothing and listened intently to the dark, depressing music. She would pierce her eyebrows and lips with safety pins as well as use black lipstick and nail polish.

"For most kids," Nixon said. "The Goth culture is a way to rebel. To control their own image. It is a relatively harmless phase for most involved. They're young. They act out. Then they grow out of it. For some kids, however, like Natasha, it is more than that. She's disturbed to begin with and wants to take it beyond the dark music and black get-ups and really wants to do harm to someone. She realized that the Goth culture was a way to make people afraid of her. This is how she would gain power. She could control people by being their 'darkness consultant.'"

NATASHA THE VAMPIRE

She became a self-described "vampire" and named her black dog "Malkavian" after the vampires in her favorite vampire fantasy board game as well as collecting all of Anne Rice's vampire novels.

"She was a dark soul who'd give you the willies," a local teen said in describing her.

Natasha covered the walls of her bedroom in her trailer with numerous dark messages including "I hate the world" as well as drawing inverted crosses.

"Tasha would start hearing voices," Wallen said. "Talking to people on the Oujia board. Her and Karen fed on each other. You know. It just kept getting worse. She wanted away from all the people that called her 'freak.'"

Her drug use and drinking increased but she was able to attract a group of friends, most of whom looked up to her. The group consisted of three girls. The petite Karen Howell and the overweight, awkward Crystal Sturgill.

Sturgill was molested by her step-father and had been kicked out of her home. She needed a place to stay and hooked up with Karen and Natasha.

The threesome would go around the sleepy Kentucky town, spray painting pentagrams, the satanic number 666 and inverted crosses across the walls of buildings and homes.

"They were all sort of drop outs," reporter Bill Jones said. "Who fell through the cracks in school. They dressed in Gothic fashion, black clothing. Black make-up. Looks Satanic, if you're looking for Satanic that's what might come to mind."

"Everything that we did," Natasha said. "Was very destructive but also self-destructive. Nothing was done to harm anybody but ourselves."

Natasha began spelling her name backwards, 'Ah-Satan', spray painting it across the walls of the town.

"She used the name to intimidate," Dixon said. "In an odd way, that was part of her charm. She was more 'out there' than the impressionable kids in her town. She held sway over Karen Howell and Crystal Sturgill, both of whom were looking for someone they could look up to. So while Natasha was an outcast at school she was able to assemble other outcasts and cast them under her spell. She became the devil of choice to worship."

The gang carried around two books with them, *The Book of Black Magic* and the *Complete Book of Magic and Witchcraft.* The three girls would go to motel rooms or Natasha's mother's trailer to hang out, drink alcohol and each other's blood. They would also engage in seances and Satanic rituals they would read about in books.

"When it comes to the occult," Dixon said. "Most young people just dabble around with it. In the case of Natasha and her gang, however, she led them over the edge. They were dumb kids out looking for kicks and she pushed them into something that they probably would not have gotten involved in had it not been for her own dark compulsions."

ROAD TRIP TO HELL

"We're going to start armageddon," Natasha informed one of her friends. "I hate, therefore I am" became her mantra.

Natasha and the "Wild Bunch" decided to go on a road trip to New Orleans. They were obsessed with the vampire books of Anne Rice and thought about the prospect of meeting her. Talks began and the entire group wanted to leave the small town of Pikeville behind.

"All I could think of was I need out," Natasha said. "I need out. I need out. I need out. I can't breathe, I need out."

The group of girls were now joined by some equally nefarious young men. The first is Joe Risner who is Karen's boyfriend and at twenty years old, the oldest in the group. Risner, never knew his own father and was known as the quiet, introverted type. He wanted to impressed Karen but was insecure as his love interest seemed more infatuated with Natasha then with him.

Edward Dean Mullins was nineteen and the only one from the group that comes from an intact family that goes to church. He is struggling with self-esteem issues, however, as women reject him until he meets Natasha. James Bryant is fourteen but seemingly the most volatile of the "Wild Bunch". His mother has abandoned him and left him alone with an alcoholic father. Natasha and Karen met him on a street corner and picked him up because they thought he looked "cool." Mostly likely, they saw him as someone the could use to do their dirty work.

"I had been friends with Joe for awhile," Natasha said. "Joe was dating Karen. Crystal needed a place to stay and she was friends with Dean (Mullins)."

Jason was the last entry into the "Wild Bunch." It was apparent, however, that he and Natasha didn't always see eye to eye. According to detectives, Jason was not as "controllable" as others in Natasha's group.

"Jason didn't make a huge impact on me," Natasha said. "He seemed dangerous. Like people pretend to be bad. I thought that was his hook. He was the 'bad boy.'"

Natasha's mother's trailer would be their primary hangout where they would drink, do drugs and later plot out their killing spree.

"Prior to leaving (for the road trip)," Bell said. "The defendants would watch 'Natural Born Killers.' That movie depicts individuals who are carefree, killing people. There don't appear to be from that movie, any consequences (to violence). They may have felt that there were not going to be any consequences for their actions. I really don't know what it takes for a group of people to take on that mentality of murder. They had no concept of tomorrow. Or consequences. And they just don't care."

The members of the gang become increasingly excited as they discuss the prospects of what will take place on their killing spree. Finally, they have some excitement in their boring, despondent lives with Natasha at the head.

"She seemed to be the leader of the group," Jones said. "And someone in the group said 'we're going to make headlines.'"

MOTEL SEVEN PIT STOP

The group piled into Risner's mother's car, a compact Chevy Citation. Before they would hit the highway, they rented out room number seven at the Colley Motel in Pikeville. Despite Natasha's apparent disdain for Jason, the young fourteen year old had cut Natasha's initials into his arm that night at the motel. The group then attempted to burn the satanic numbers 666 into the motel carpet with candle wax.

They would then begin their self-mutilation ritual.

"Me and Karen started cutting," Natasha said. "And at first, it was just to cut. Then I wanted to die. I thought eventually if I cut myself so many times I would just bleed out. Mostly it was just me and Karen drinking each others blood. We just didn't do seances."

Crystal maintains that they were not part of a vampire cult or nor did they worship Satan. "We dressed in black and we'd stand out. And we did self-multilation. We were the freaks, the outcasts."

"We were trying to find answers, " Crystal said during in interview with Campus Life. "We all had been to church. It didn't provide answers. We were interested in Wicca, books on witches and spells. We were anarchists."

"They wanted to go to New Orleans," Natasha said. "Because that was the only place I was familiar with. And I said I wouldn't go back down there without some kind of protection."

Natasha was referring to the fact that she claimed to be raped in New Orleans although no charges were filed.

The motel owner, Jim Cochran, said that he rented out the room to Risner and described him as "polite and courteous". Risner, who also wore the Goth black make-up was described by detectives as "lanky and long-haired." A week before their killing spree, Natasha was in a Pikeville grocery store where she led Risner around by a dog chain fastened to a collar around his neck.

The group started a fire in the motel room and they were worried the manager would call the cops.

"Karen had just gotten into trouble," Natasha said. "And she didn't want to go back to juvenile. Jason just got out of juvenile and he didn't want to go back. And I was ready to run away at any given moment so it just kinda came together. We were all going to run away."

The group then vandalized and burglarized other Colley Motel rooms during their stay. They stole a television set and several pairs of work boots.

ROUTE 666

The group of disaffected youth drove to Forty-Acre Field, a remote campground where other teens would hang out. They started a campfire then at some point that night or early in the morning they burglarized two homes in a town called Paintsville. It was there they stole two semi-automatic handguns.

They thought about performing a carjacking as Joe's mother's Chevy Citation kept overheating. Nonetheless, they went onto U.S. Highway 23 south into Virginia.

The group was ticketed for speeding in Gate City, Virginia on April 6th but were allowed to continue on.

"Based on the evidence of what their stated purpose was," Bell said. "The night before they left. They were preparing to leave Pikeville. Go across the country. Robbing and killing people."

The group then drove into a used car lot and tried unsuccessfully to hot wire a vehicle.

They kept driving and an hour later, they stopped at the Interstate Highway 81 rest stop in Greeneville, Tennessee.

"Karen needed to pee," Natasha said.

Tragedy would ensue as the group came upon the Lillelid family at a truck stop in Greeneville,

THE LILLELID FAMILY

Thirty-four year old Norwegian Vidar Lillelid, his twenty-eight year old wife Delfina, their six year old daughter Tabitha and two year old son Peter were having lunch on a park bench.

Vidar, who worked as a hotel bellman, had taken his family to a religious convention in Johnson City. They were on their way home to Nashville. He had been in the USA for ten years. His wife, Delfina was a native of New Jersey but had parents who had immigrated from Honduras. The two had married in 1989 and moved to Knoxville four years earlier from Miami because they wanted a nice place to raise their two children. The two were described as "devoutly faithful" and "humble" by those who knew them.

"The Jehovah's Witnesses were having a convention abut thirty miles north," Jones recalled. "They had been to that convention and they were going home. Jehovah Witnesses are known for being active in trying to recruit new members. They leave pamphlets and that sort of thing. That may have been the worst thing they could have done."

"I think they were doing a little proselytizing there," Bell said. "It was just part of their religion that they go out and try and talk to people. They saw the defendant's unusual appearance. They may have though that they needed some discussion about the Lord."

Vidar and Delfina approached the group and asked if they believed in God. Natasha spoke for the everyone, saying she dd not believe in God, as he had never come to her aid when she prayed as a child.

"The whole scenario just drips with tragic irony," Dixon said. "On one hand, we have the Lillelid family. They are sweet and naïve. They are following the dictates of their church to go out and invite as many members as they can for their church. Then there are these cult members who a diametrically opposed viewpoint. They have their own beliefs. Only theirs are something far more sinister."

KIDNAPPING AT GUNPOINT

According to Natasha, it was Joe who initiated the kidnapping of the family.

"It was when Joe said he wanted to converse with Vidar about his religious beliefs," Natasha said. "That just brought up red flags, because Joe was not a religious man. I tried to convince him (Joe) that we should just leave and get on our own way. Every step that he took, I was there trying to prevent it."

Natasha stated that it was never their intent to rob and kill the Lillelids. She became alarmed with Joe who went back to his car and got his gun. Then after conversing with Jason, Joe pulled the gun out on the Lillelids.

Detectives confirmed that Joe Risner admitted that he was the one that pulled the gun. Natasha remained steadfast in her own statement that she tried to stop Joe.

"He was like 'nothing is gonna happen,'" Natasha said. "'We just need your car.' All I could do was just look at them and apologize."

Vidar immediately offered his keys and wallet, pleading for the killers to not harm his family.

"They put them in their respective cars and took off," Bell said. "They got off the Interstate. Just a few miles down the road."

"I didn't think that the people that I was around could actually do anything bad," Natasha said. "Even Jason. I thought I could stop something."

Detectives found out otherwise, however. During interviews with the other members of the group, they believed that Natasha was the instigator. She was the one that members of the group thought could "draw on demons" and was the driving force behind the robbery.

Joseph Risner forced the family into the Citation. They drove along until they reach a remote area.

"It's a dead end, gravel, one lane road," Jones said. "They go down the end of that road and force the people out of the car."

The family is terrified. Vidar continued to plead for mercy. Young Peter is clinging to his mother's leg, his arms wrapped tight around her waist.

"This group of very strange looking people is surrounding them and laughing," Bell said. "And they see the weapon."

"I can't imagine what that would have been like," Jones said. "To know that your family was in peril like that."

According to Natasha, it was Risner that pulled the gun on the family but now on the deserted road it was Jason Bryant, the fourteen year old, who held the family at gunpoint.

"All of a sudden Jason pulled the gun up," Natasha said. "All I could see was rage on his face. And Joe walked away from it. He was like, 'I can't do that.' And I was like 'Jason, what are you doing? And he just started cussing. 'Get the fuck outta the way! Get the fuck outta the way! Move! Unless you wanna die, move!

"I got in between Jason and the family to where the gun was pointed at me and tried to convince him to not do that. I begged and I pleaded for what seemed like an eternity for him to stop. When I discovered that there was no stopping him, I begged for at least the children to be saved. He told me that if I didn't move, he would shoot me."

"I don't think I would have moved anyway until he promised and swore to me that he would not harm the children. That's when I moved. I didn't think that I could do anything to prevent it if I was dead."

During the testimony, Natasha, Risner and Karen Howell said that Bryant did the shooting. Bryant, however, said that Risner and Edward Dean Mullins fired the shots and later forced him to take the blame.

Gunpowder was found on Mullins, however. The detectives and prosecuting attorney believed that the entire group somehow were involved in the shootings as over seventeen shots were fired.

"If you wanted to be a member of this group," Bell said. "You had to participate in this ritualistic killing."

"I don't know which (of the family) got shot first," Bell said. "But the rest of them are observing their family being shot."

"The indication was that the children were shot last," Jones said. "The little girl had apparently walked around in her mother's blood. The boy even though he was two years old was shot in the head."

"I didn't watch," Natasha claimed. "I sat in the back of the van and just screamed. Please don't hurt them. Please don't hurt them. Please don't hurt them. Jason said 'Stop fucking crying.' He just laughed."

Six year old Tabitha was shot in the head. Peter was being held by his mother as he was shot. Each of the victim was shot in the eye as a 'signature' move.

"The males were shot in the right eye," Bell said. "And the women on the left."

"It was a ritualized killing," Dixon said. "Call it bonding through murder. They would hoop and holler and cheer each other on. "

The group left Risner's mother's car at the scene as it became stuck in the mud. They stole the family's van, the youths took off in the hopes of going to Mexico.

But not before they had dragged the bodies over, lying the four bodies parallel to each other so it appeared like a four-pointed star.

Joe laughed as they drove over the bodies, hearing the crunch of bone under the weight of the van.

THE AFTERMATH

Vidar and Delfina were found dead, tire tracks across their clothing. Tabitha was still alive when found but died en route to the hospital. Two year old Peter was shot in the torso and the eye. Amazingly, the boy survived although he is now blind in one eye and permanently disabled.

"Peter survived," Jones said. "The two year old boy had been shot through the eye with the bullet exiting the side of his head. It didn't kill him. He's disabled by the extent of his injuries. He had difficulty walking and of course, blind in one eye.

The youths showed no remorse after the shooting. People who lived nearby heard gunshots, laughing and shouting as they left the family for dead. The police were called and the Sheriffs discovered the dead bodies of the Lillelid family.

ON THE RUN

"After you witness something that atrocious," Natasha said. "I didn't know what to do."

The group went on the run, altering their plans to go to New Orleans. Instead, they headed to Arizona/Mexico border.

Two days after the shootings, Natasha and her cohorts were arrested by US Customs and Immigration officials in Arizona.

"They had been down into Mexico," Bell said. "And as they were coming back through the computers at the border had not been functioning. So the border could not check on who was coming in and out. But just as that group came back in the computer suddenly started working. And when they put the license tag in the system they got a hit. And they were arrested there in Arizona."

The detectives and defense attorney who dealt with Natasha after the arrest vary widely from her own well-thought versions of what took place that night.

"She was a vampire who worshiped Satan," said an officer who spoke to Natasha after her arrest. "She was on the dark side. Very bitter towards everyone."

Natasha allegedly told her first defense attorney, Eric Conn, that she was 'Satan's Daughter.' The attorney decided to play up that aspect of her defense as he hoped to get her a lenient sentence if she was declared insane.

"After Eric Conn got up in the devil worship and vampirism," Wallen said. "It kept getting worse and worse."

Natasha blames her first lawyer, Conn, for her lackluster defense.

"I don't know why it was me that was picked out of everyone else," Natasha said. "I know he did a lot of damage to me and my case.

"I didn't tell him that I even had any inclination toward that," Natasha recalled. "I knew he was a lawyer wanting to represent me pro bono. At no point had I ever been a satanist. Ever. Once something like that is said. You can't just take it back."

Conn was later replaced by Stacy Street but the damage had been done.

Natasha's current court-appointed attorney stated that "he (Conn) volunteered to represent her, then immediately began negotiating movie rights.

SOUVENIRS OF A KILL

"Each one of these killers," Berkeley said. "Took an individual trophy from their victims. And kept it attached to a chain or a wallet."

Karen Howell took Vidar's social security card and Tabitha's 'Hello Kitty' merchandise. Natasha took Tabitha's social security card and her wallet. Sturgill had taken the keys to the Lillelid home all for souvenirs.

DEATH PENALTY?

"We were very concerned that the proof might focus on the juveniles as being the shooters," Bell said. "Juveniles can't get the death penalty. And if they can't get the death penalty we were concerned that no one else would get the death penalty either. What we reached was an agreement that we'd have a hearing."

A media circus followed the trial as an angry mob descended upon the teenagers as they entered the courtroom.

"Someone yelled that I was Charles Manson's daughter," recalled Sturgill.

In the trial, all six defendants had different stories as to how events took place that night and who pulled the trigger.

"It is my position that it was part of an initiation," Bell said. "That everybody had to participate in the shooting."

"Natasha clearly was the ring leader in all of the killings here," Dixon said. "She was the most articulate and confident of the group. The young men in the group were all shy types, eager from some female validation, with the possible exception of Jason who was a budding psychopath. But again, he was a dim-witted fourteen year old pitted against a smooth-talker in Natasha. Sturgill and Howell looked up to Natasha in their own ways as well. Sturgill was social awkward, overweight. She finally found people she could call friends and would do whatever they said. And Karen would not become violent on her own. These individuals were all like that, they could be violent but needed someone to light the fuse. And Natasha struck the match for everyone.

CONVICTION

Natasha was convicted on March 13th, 1998 with the five other youths. She reached a plea bargain where she plead guilty to all of the charges to avoid the death penalty.

In her court testimony, Natasha maintained that she was not the shooter of the four victims. She kept asserting that she tried to prevent the deaths of the Lillelid family members.

All of the defendants were sentenced to three life terms plus twenty-five years without the possibility of parole.

"She wasn't the shooter," Natasha's mother said, maintaining her daughter's innocence. "She got the same thing as the shooter."

PRISON LIFE

Natasha is housed at a prison in Nashville. She has earned her GED and her mother Madonna claims that her daughter serves as a "mentor to fellow inmates as they work to earn their GED."

"I was a teacher's aide for about a year," Natasha said during a newspaper interview.

Her troubled times continued, however, as on August of 24th 2001, she and death row inmate Christa Pike allegedly attacked a fellow prisoner named Patricia Jones.

They tried to strangle Jones to death with a shoe string after all three were placed in a holding cell with Natasha during a fire alarm.

Pike was on death row for torturing and beating a woman to death when they were Job Corps students in 1995.

Another inmate, the twenty-year old Jennifer Szostecki started the fire which created confusion during the fire alarm. This allowed Christa Pike to gain access to Patricia Jones.

Jones allegedly teased Pike about her upcoming execution.

"All she does is snitch on me and stab me in the back," Pike said during a phone call with her mother.

Natasha allegedly struggled with Jones before Pike came from behind and started to choke Jones with the shoe strings from a hiking boot. Natasha was Pike's friend and Szostecki's "girlfriend."

Letters filed in criminal court show Szostecki's obsession with Natasha.

"I love you," Sozstecki wrote. "I hate you. I miss you. I want you. I need you."

Pike was later charged with attempted murder while there was insufficient evidence to charge Natasha.

"I expected big women with shanks and stuff like that," Natasha said of her time in prison. "You know, like that typical prison scene that you would see in a movie. But it's not like that. You just get up, go to meals, have an hour out for recreational purposes and watch television and read."

PETER LILLELID

Peter Lillelid would be the subject of a custody battle between his USA based relatives and his aunt in Sweden. His aunt and uncle from Sweden won custody and Peter was sent to be in their care.

They kept him shielded from the media and he does not like to read the accounts of what happened to his parents and sister.

A MOTHER'S KILLER : THE TRUE STORY OF NICOLE KASINSKAS

CHRISTINE GOODMAN

Nicole Kasinskas was a quiet, unassuming teenage girl. She was born and raised in Nashua, New Hampshire to Anthony Kasinskas and Jeanne Domenico.

"I lived with both of my parents and my younger brother until I was eleven years old," Nicole said. "And my parents divorced and my Dad moved out."

"I think after my parents got divorced and I was dealing with that, I became a little bit angrier. I had a little bit more resentment towards him, and it did change my perspectives about myself and about life in general, I guess even as an eleven year old."

In May of 2002, she found "romance" as a fifteen year old on-line with eighteen-year old Billy Sullivan.

Sullivan lived in a town called Willmantic where he worked as a line cook at McDonald's.

"Nicole hadn't had a lot of boyfriends," prosecuting attorney Kirsten Wilson said . "She was really caught up by the attention by this guy who was saying amazing things to her about how beautiful she was and what she meant to him."

They would communicate daily through e-mail, letters and phone calls. Despite not having met in person, they both declared love for each other within days, speaking of marriage and planning their future together.

"They filled in sort of the gaps of everyday communication and relationships with fantasies and making these assumptions on who the other person was," Wilson said.

"He lived in Connecticut and so our relationship was almost one hundred percent over the phone," Nicole said. "But it became everything to me very quickly because of the amount of attention that he paid me, and I didn't really feel that I was getting that from anywhere else."

Nicole had been vulnerable to Sullivan's Internet advances as she was a loner with very few friends in high school. She was routinely bullied at school by other girls. On one occasion, she was walking down the hall and one of her bullies had pulled her sweatpants down to her ankles. Nicole was not wearing any underwear, furthering the humiliation. Nicole refused to go back to school the next day after that incident.

"The bullying at school certainly made Nicole vulnerable to someone like Sullivan," forensic psychologist Fiona Russo said. "She's lonely, she's being picked on at school and completely humiliated. She stuck to herself and so when some guy pays attention to her, even when it is only online, her fantasy life goes into overdrive. She's able to project things on him that he doesn't deserve or merit."

The more severe the bullying became, the more Nicole began to withdraw and cling to Sullivan.

"As I got older, it was easier for me to isolate from people," Nicole said. "I think at that point I had just gotten used to being more alone as opposed to being around people. And it just became a part of who I was. Maybe if I was more open or maybe if someone had tried harder to reach out, that it could've been different."

Nicole's mom, Jeanne, was her best friend. Jeanne worked at an elementary school for a period of time, holding down such jobs as a crossing guard, a lunchroom monitor, and a paraprofessional for about three years before taking a job where she worked on group contracts for the Benefits, Brokers and Administration department.

"Jeanne Domenico was well loved in the community," Wilson said. "Hard worker. Really sort of a bright, energetic, sweet woman. She was trying to make her daughter happy."

Despite the bullying at school, Nicole got straight A's at school and made her mother happy whenever she made the honor roll.

"School really became my self-worth and I really identified with, like whatever my grades were," Nicole said. "However I was doing in school I felt it reflected on me personally, because I felt that it was so much a part of who I was. I never got in trouble in middle school. I never got spoken to. I never had a detention. It never really crossed my mind to do anything that would be against the rules."

"It would have been helpful if there was more of an acknowledgment that I was doing so well. I think it also would've been helpful if there was more involvement with guidance or something. Just more of a like a check-in...see how things are going."

"Somehow, someway, Nicole got lost in the cracks," Russo said. "That in no way justifies what she did. It may be how she justified it during this time. Her parents are divorced. She doesn't see her Dad. Her mom is working all the time. There had to have been days where she felt intense loneliness Going to school just to be ignored or bullied. To a fourteen year old girl you really may not see the light at the end of the tunnel. So you seek an outlet. Some turn to drugs. Nicole found her own drug in the form of the words that came out of Sullivan's keyboard."

MOTHER AND DAUGHTER TROUBLES

At least on the surface, there were no problems between mother and daughter.

Until Nicole ventured on-line and met Billy Sullivan.

Her mother found out about the relationship and wanting to make her daughter happy, drove the young teenager out to Connecticut so she could meet Sullivan for the first time.

"This was a two hour drive from Nashua to the place in Connecticut where Sullivan lived," Russo said. "It is easy to say here is where Jeanne made a fatal mistake. But in her mind, it is all innocent. Her daughter is fourteen and begging her to drive out to meet this guy. Begging and begging. Until she finally she relents."

More visits followed but friends and classmates knew little of the teen's relationship. Sullivan had informed some of his friends that he had a girlfriend that was "out of state." Other than that, he revealed very little about his personal life.

"He's quiet, he didn't really like to talk," recalled Danny Goss who was a classmate of Sullivan. "But he was good in school and didn't get in any trouble."

"I think the relationship intensified to a degree that Jeanne herself didn't anticipate," Russo said. "And it is easy to play Monday morning quarterback here but there had to have been some kind of father figure present to say 'hey, this is an eighteen-year old working at McDonald's. You are a fourteen year old honor student. You have a future. Don't blow it on this guy. But it isn't like teens listen to you anyway."

The two teenagers soon discussed the prospect of moving in together. Her mother quickly objected to this idea as well as nixing the idea of Nicole sharing a joint bank account with Sullivan.

But the young man later stayed overnight one weekend with Nicole's mother's full consent.

The relationship is the first for Nicole. She pedestalizes Sullivan as everything she has fantasized about is coming true.

"Nicole had a void in her life," Russo said. "When her parents divorced it certainly affected her psychologically in the way she viewed men. Then along comes Sullivan whose older and more experienced. She gets the love from him that perhaps she sought from her father. The older man, wiser than his years, showering her with attention. She was vulnerable to that."

"Her father didn't have too much to do with her after the divorce. She had that longing in her heart for that male figure. And along came Sullivan."

PERSONAL DEMONS OF HIS OWN

Sullivan, however, had his own personal demons he was fighting.

"He did have mental health issues," Wilson said. "He had been hospitalized a number of times. During high school he had some behavioral issues. Some anxiety, that kind of thing."

It was later revealed that Sullivan had been on numerous psychiatric medications to curb his depression, anger and schizophrenia. He had been weaning himself off the meds, however, and on one occasion he engaged in an argument with Nicole's mother over dinner.

Jeanne had asked Billy if she liked the dinner she had prepared. He said yes and then Jean made the comment that "I bet you don't get that too much at home."

Sullivan was highly defensive over anything that involved his home life. When Jeanne made that comment, he turned hostile.

"Sullivan was protective of his home life," Russo said. "If anyone insulted his mother or if he even perceives that someone is insulting his mother then he gets abusive. He did this to Jeanne, who had obviously made nothing more than an idle comment. That was the first warning sign and the relationship should have ended then and there."

Nicole, however, defended her young beau and from that moment the tug of war for her heart began.

"Nicole's own naivete comes to bore at this point," Russo said. "She has no experience with boys and here is this older guy that she looks up to, almost as a father figure of sorts, who turns her against her own family. Against the one person who loved her the most. Her mother. It is a tug of war that the mother loses simply because her daughter's hormones are raging and she doesn't yet have the emotional capacity to know any better."

After a year of dating, in August of 2003, Sullivan drove out to Nashua to spend a week with Nicole. By this time, they are both fed up with Nicole's mother's objections to their ideas of cohabitation.

"Our relationship was definitely emotionally abusive," Nicole said. "And I think now over time, from looking at it, my perspectives on that have changed so much. I feel like he is responsible for his actions and I am responsible for mine. I didn't really get that and I feel like in order to be emotionally abused, in order to stand for it and stay in it, there's gotta be something missing in you. There's gotta be something hurting already, something is not there, something's not right. And that needs to be figured out, found and fixed. Regardless of how a child is acting or what's coming off,there's more inside that kids need help with or guidance or just to have some type of connection with someone. You need to have relationships with people ahead of time, so that when the bad stuff does happen does happen you don't just come in to it expecting to work it out. Like, you need to have firm foundation with that person in order to work it out."

Nicole continued to side with Sullivan against her mother. The two argued constantly, Sullivan's influence quickly become apparent in Nicole's attitude toward her mother as she found fault with everything she did.

The two teens began discussing an unheard of option.

They began discussing the prospect of killing her mother.

"Well, this is where it starts getting...it's a scary business for me," Nicole said in a jailhouse interview. "I'll tell you that. I feel like I"m gonna cry. I don't talk about this stuff so this is really the first time. I think that my relationship with my mom was good. It was fine. I loved my mom. And...that changed. When...I'm not saying I stopped loving my mom, but...our relationship changed. I'm not gonna say that we were the most open because we weren't. We didn't talk about every little thing. I don't remember ever once talking about my parents' divorce with either of them. But the thing is, we didn't really talk about much of anything. When I was fourteen, I became involved with seventeen year old boy. This is really stemming into why I'm here (in jail) now."

OUT OF CONTROL

"Emotions begin to run high as Sullivan ups the ante in his hatred for Nicole's mother," Russo said. "Nicole is emotionally underdeveloped and has to choose between her mother and her 'man.' It is easy to look at it hindsight but with the teenaged girl's warp logic, she sees Sullivan as her entire world now. So she will do anything for him. Even murder."

Nicole's mom really didn't realize the danger that Sullivan was. She began doing what every mom does, demanding that her daughter stop seeing him, stop chatting with him and concentrate on her schoolwork. Nicole, on the other hand, remained fervent in her desire to move to Connecticut to move in with Sullivan.

"Jeanie, rightfully so, said 'you're fifteen you're finishing school,'" Wilson said. "'You're not moving to Connecticut' and that really upset both Nicole and Billy."

The prospect of not seeing Nicole had an adverse emotional effect on Billy.

"He started talking about killing himself...on the road...driving into a big truck because of leaving me..because of his sadness over it," Nicole recalled. "And I think now it just sounds silly, you know? But it wasn't then, and it was terrifying to me because I didn't...I didn't know how to...because of the way that our relationship was. Because he had become so much a part of my life. I mean, I really didn't feel like I was anything without him. I had nothing in my life at that time...I felt...at that time. So the thought of losing him in that way just wasn't okay with me. And that is unfortunately when conversations started about ultimately what happened. I guess I really I don't really go into too many details but I was sixteen and he was eighteen at that time. And I guess I should give you some background. He killed my mom and I was a part of it. I was not physically there but I knew and I helped him. I was, you know, going through the motions of what was being done. But mentally and emotionally, I don't think I was fully there. I don't think I was fully getting it."

"It was emotional manipulation," Russo said. "It is all so scary romantic for a fifteen year old girl to have some guy who is so in love with her that he is going to kill himself because he can't be with her. She has no one in her life to say 'this guy is a loser nutcase.' There isn't anyone that can talk sense to her. So she falls for the emotional manipulation of a highly disturbed but cunning con man."

Billy had convinced the depressed Nicole that her mother was an obstacle to both hers and his happiness.

"I really just did whatever I could to maintain that relationship because I didn't want to lose that," Nicole said. "I didn't want to lose him. And I quickly learned how it would go if I didn't always do everything that he wanted me to do. At that point...you know, getting to be fifteen...sixteen years old...I would fight more with my mom and there was a lot more to fight about, especially with, you know, this relationship that I was having with this kid."

THE FINAL PLAN

The couple tried different methods to murder Jeanne Domenico.

First they tried to poison Jeanne's coffee. The teens had placed Dimetapp, Benadryl and other drugs into Jeanne's coffee creamer in the refrigerator.

Jeanne used the creamer but didn't die and evidently remained ignorant of the plot on her life. The teens then added bleach to the creamer, wanting to strengthen the amount of poison. It was unclear in a court affidavit if Jeanne ever drank from the spiked creamer again.

The next idea was to set Nicole's mattress on fire with a candle. That idea didn't work because the bedding was made of fire retardant material.

It is unclear how the teens planned to fire up the mattress, whether they sneaked into her Nicole's bedroom and tried to fire up the mattress while she slept.

The third idea was to blow up the fuel oil tank in Jeanne's house. The teens had tied two ropes together which would serve as a wick. Their idea was to set fire to the rope which would then ignite a fire from the fuel tank. This idea was of course unsuccessful.

"These were hair-brained schemes from the start," Russo said, "particularly the fuel tank episode. What is interesting is that these are passive attacks. There is no face to face encounter with the mother, they just really want her gone. But it does show how these were test-runs of sorts. Sullivan was working up his nerve to do something violent. Nicole was building up her psyche. With each unsuccessful dry run, their determination and focus to do the job became greater until finally they realized that physical violence would be the only alternative."

THE ATTACK

The couple decided that Sullivan would do the killing. Nicole waited in the car at a local 7-Eleven where he mother worked part time to make ends meet. She wanted to wait there because she hated her home so much. Her boyfriend obliged, and entered the home of Jeanne Domenico between the hours of six and seven in the evening, waiting for her to come home from work.

The plan was for Billy to kill Jeanne by hitting her on the back of her head with a baseball bat.

Nicole waited anxiously in the car for an extended period of time then began to get worried as to why Sullivan was taking so long.

"Nicole called him and asked him what was taking so long," Wilson said. "Jeanne began getting upset that Nicole wasn't home and kept saying 'where is she? Tell her to come home.'"

Nicole heard her mother's voice on the other end of her cell phone telling her to "come home."

As became her habit, she did not listen to her mother.

"Sullivan did not attack Jeanne immediately," Russo said. "Again, he needed that fuel to add to his fire. So he confronted Jeanne, asking her why they kept refusing them to be together. Jeanne would speak logically like any adult would. She's underage. She's still in school. Of course, none of this would get into the head of Sullivan."

Jeanne made the mistake of turning her back on the young man. He then hit her across the back with the baseball bat.

"It looks as if Jeanne tried to get out of the kitchen door," Wilson said. "Billy started grabbing kitchen knives and attacking Jeanne with the steak knives from the state clock in the kitchen."

The attack was, in a word, brutal.

Sullivan stabbed Jeanne numerous times near her heart and stomach. He stabbed with such ferocity that the blade broke off the knife and he had to retrieve another. Then he stabbed her eight times in the throat.

"A number of the steak knives snapped off during the course of the attack," Wilson said.

According to later testimony by Sullivan, Jeanne managed to get a hold of one of the knives and tried to fight back. At this point, however, she is stunned and bleeding. Sullivan realizes that he is in trouble and goes in to finish the job.

Sullivan stabs her repeatedly as Jeanne tries to get away. A blade enters her lung.

"I'm done," were Jeanne's final words.

He then changed his clothes and cleaned the blood off. He then went back to Nicole, telling her to go inside the house to check for any weapons that he may have left behind. He also told her to get a towel.

The murder complete, Sullivan returned to the vehicle and announced that he had done the deal.

The couple, however, had a deal. It was now time for Nicole to do her part. She would help clean up the evidence left behind.

"The fact that she could go and clean up after Billy had killed her mother," Wilson said. "She had to have hit her mother with the door. And then she had to have stepped over her body to clean up for her boyfriend. That she was able to do that was chilling to do me."

Nicole took a cloth and began clean up her mother's blood from the kitchen floor.

"The fact that a psychopath like Sullivan was able to stab Jeanne to death isn't the most blood curdling aspect of this case," Russo said. "The really scary part is how Nicole was able to go back into that house, see her mother laying in a pool of blood on the kitchen floor, then begin to do her end of the bargain, which was to clean up after her boyfriend. The amount of psychological and emotional disconnect here is chilling."

The two then hid the evidence in the outskirts around town before going to a shopping mall in order for Sullivan to purchase new clothes.

Hours after the killing, Nicole finally began to realize the gravity of what has taken place. She realizes that she and Billy were not going off to "see the world." Her best friend, her mother was gone forever.

Jeanne's body would be discovered by her boyfriend later that evening and he quickly called the police. At around 10:15 p.m., Sergeant William Moore and Detective Shawn Hill saw Sullivan and Nicole approach the crime scene.

"They were cocky enough to think they could outwit the cops," Russo said. "By approaching the crime scene and acting all innocent, not knowing what happened, they thought they would deflect attention away from themselves. It really shows you how dumb these two kids were."

The police then stated the teens would have to be separated for an interview. Nicole protested, stating that Sullivan would not know how to get to the police station. The police informed her that they would take him there themselves.

"This is when things start to go haywire in their heads," Russo said. "Nicole is getting nervous, knowing that they will be questioned separately and face the prospect of not having their stories straight. These two were not exactly forward thinking individuals."

The two waited for the police cruisers to arrive and made conversation with Detective Moore. The detective noted that Sullivan did most all of the talking and admitted that he did not like police officers, stating that he had been charged before with crimes he did not commit.

Moore informed Sullivan that he would be given a "fair shake" in the questioning.

Sullivan, however, kept talking. He informed the detective that he had been shopping for souvenirs with Nicole that day and talked about Jeanne's relationship with Nicole. The detective said that Sullivan paced back and forth and then sat down on the trunk of his car.

Twelve minutes later, Detective Linehan arrived on the scene, making contact with both Nicole and Sullivan. Linehan noticed how nervous and "jumpy" Sullivan was. Linehan told Sullivan to "relax" and then the teen explained that he suffered from anxiety but did not need medication. He told the police that he had "no problem" to come to the station for questioning.

Linehan sat with Sullivan in the back seat of the squad car as they headed back to the station. Both of the teens were having casual conversations with the officers but after being questioned separately, they both admitted their involvement, leading police to the locations where they had disposed of the evidence.

"Both of the teenage lovers wilted under the police interrogations," Russo said. "She immediately ratted out Sullivan as the killer while he did the same to her. There was no loyalty for one another while under the police questioning."

Sullivan would be convicted of first degree murder, sentenced to life without parole.

Sullivan, however, did not let his Lothario ways go to rust in jail. He wrote love letters to a girl named Monique Teal who was then sixteen. This occurred while Sullivan was awaiting trial and later Teal's testimony was used in court.

Teal, using a pen name of Monique Sullivan in her love letters to Sullivan, had agreed to a date to marry the now twenty-year old murderer. Teal's mother, however, found out about the letters and forbade him to call or write.

"He just laughed about it," she said. "He said that no matter what my mom would say or do that nothing could keep us away from each other."

"You see him trying the same techniques on Teal," Russo said. "The immediate declarations of love. The flowery language. The idea of them against the world. In Teal's case, however, her mother put a stop to it."

Sullivan admitted to the Jeanne Domenico killing in one of his letters to her, Teal would reveal, although she didn't read from the letter in court. She said she obeyed Sullivan's demands and threw that letter away.

JAIL LIFE

Nicole Kasinskas would plead guilty to second-degree murder.

"My original sentence was forty years to life," Nicole said. "It is now thirty-seven years and a half to life based on a plea that if I acquired my GED I would get two and a half years off. I don't mark days off on my calendar. I don't do those types of things. This is my life now and I want to live it. I don't want to just look at it as one day down closer to my real life. Like this is my real life. I smile a lot and I live a lot and I'm happy a lot and I just prefer it that way rather than get lost in the sadness of it because you can. And I have. But if I...if I can choose not to...if I can be stronger than than then I want to. And it makes me feel freer. It makes me feel that I have more control of my life."

"Her life as a promising honor roll student at fifteen years old with her mother who loved her very much," Wilson said. "She lost her entire life. And for what?"

"I had no goals. I had no hopes and dreams, you know? You need to have your own hobbies and friends and stuff. Outside the relationship, there needs to be that balance. I just never had that, I never figured that out."

"Maybe if someone had said something like, 'I see you, I see that there's more to you than this and I want to see more of you. I'm here for you. I care about you.' I mean everyone needs help, everyone needs support."

Milton Keynes UK
Ingram Content Group UK Ltd.
UKHW012051260524
443218UK00001BA/81